This Is Our Writing

T.F. RIGELHOF
This Is Our Writing

with photographs by Gabor Szilasi

The Porcupine's Quill

CANADIAN CATALOGUING IN PUBLICATION DATA

Rigelhof, T.F.
This is our writing

ISBN 0-88984-218-3

1. Canadian literature (English) – 20th century – History and criticism.
I. Szilasi, Gabor, 1928– . II. Title.

PS8071.4.R53 2000   C810.9'0054   C00-932171-3
PR9189.6.R53 2000

Published by The Porcupine's Quill,
68 Main Street, Erin, Ontario NOB 1TO.
Readied for the press by John Metcalf; copy edited by Doris Cowan.
Typeset in Minion, printed on Zephyr Antique laid,
and bound at The Porcupine's Quill Inc.

Represented in Canada by the Literary Press Group.
Trade orders are available from General Distribution Services.

We acknowledge the support of the Ontario Arts Council,
and the Canada Council for the Arts for our publishing program.
The financial support of the Government of Canada
through the Book Publishing Industry Development Program
is also gratefully acknowledged.

1 2 3 4 · 02 01 00

Canada

for my mother Katherine
and for her other children, my sisters and brother –
Gloria, Leona, Isabella, Marina, Dolli, Damaris and Roger

And, always, for Ann

Acknowledgements

This collection began with my efforts to show why John Irving and so many others are simply wrong about Robertson Davies and why Leonard Cohen's first novel *The Favourite Game* is so splendidly and gloriously right in what it does. Those articles were commissioned by Bev Daurio of *Paragraph* magazine. John Metcalf spotted them and, renewing an earlier acquaintance, suggested I write a book of such essays, on other Canadian writers I admired or deplored. John encouraged me to write the pieces I saw fit as I puzzled to make sense of what is best in some of the books Canadians have made in English. He also served as my editor. I've benefited from his good sense and literary instincts in more ways than I can count and I can count beyond my fingers and toes. Given that John works as ardently to collect, preserve and promote the best of our past as he does to solicit new books, it's not surprising that other books he has edited get mentioned in this one: he has my thanks not just for what he has done on behalf of this book but, especially, for what he has done to keep Hugh Hood's *Around the Mountain* and Norman Levine's *Canada Made Me* in print.

Bits and pieces from some of my output as a reviewer of books have been incorporated into these larger pieces. My thanks to past and present editors of the books sections of the *Montreal Gazette*, the *Ottawa Citizen*, the *Toronto Star* and the *Globe and Mail* extend far beyond the re-use I've made of words written originally for their papers. I particularly want to thank Martin Levin and Jack Kirchhoff at the *Globe and Mail* for continuing to push my reading in directions it might not otherwise travel.

Like all my others, this book carries the name of Ann, my constant companion, on the dedication page. I don't think that even she realizes how much her reading means to mine. Ann works in a public library where she does much to publicize new books and delights in bringing together the right book and the right reader. Ann believes in public service and describes books with a precision and concision that's a marvel. Without her daily conversation, my life would be much poorer, my knowledge of British and American authors much scantier, my writing much thinner and everything about me much, much scattier. This does not imply that my judgements are hers or hers are mine: opposites do attract.

My friend and neighbour Gabor Szilasi, one of the artistic treasures of this country, has provided some previously unpublished photographs. I'm honoured by the presence of his work in these pages and flattered by the photographs he's taken of this author.

Finally, my thanks to all who write what I have read and to those like J and B (not the whisky guys) who have read what I've written elsewhere and here in earlier drafts and who have provided necessary criticisms: it's unfair to name names since my judgements remain stubbornly my own. I do want to record my debt to the late Matt Cohen who commented on 'George Grant at McMaster' while illness pressed in on him: Matt, to the end, was humble about his own work, though he had earned the right not to be.

As this book developed, the suggestion of a sequel kept insinuating itself, a book that will say much more than I do here about the writers whose current work I think ought to dominate discussions of Canadian writing at the beginning of a new century. Stay tuned.

Table of Contents

We know who we are, don't we? We're not Them.
— Lenny Bruce

Never use the word 'we' unless you know who you're collectivizing and are willing to kiss them on the mouth — and mean it.
— Brian Fawcett,
Unusual Circumstances, Interesting Times

Grosvenor Avenue, East Side, 1999

This Is Our Writing

(Ornette & Me & Embraceable You)

Books matter. They surely do. In themselves. They are:

> valuable, valuable like a jewel, or a lovely picture, into which you
> can look deeper and deeper and get a more profound experience
> each time. It is far, far better to read one book six times, at
> intervals, than to read six several books. Because if a certain book
> can call you to read it six times, it will be a deeper and deeper
> experience each time, and will enrich the whole soul, emotional
> and mental. Whereas six books read once only are merely an
> accumulation of superficial interest, the burdensome accumula-
> tion of modern days, quantity without real value.

So says D.H. Lawrence at the beginning of his last book *Apocalypse* –
so say I, not because Lawrence was Lawrence but because I am I, a reader
of many books once only and some few more often because I have yet to
fully fathom them: Mavis Gallant's *From the Fifteenth District*, Mordecai
Richler's *St. Urbain's Horseman*, Norman Levine's *Canada Made Me*,
Hugh Hood's *Around the Mountain*. Lawrence again:

> Once a book is fathomed, once it is *known*, and its meaning is
> fixed or established, it is dead. A book only lives while it has
> power to move us, and move us *differently*; so long as we find it
> *different* every time we read it.

I'm thinking of how very different *The Apprenticeship of Duddy
Kravitz* was on second reading as I looked for the first time at a life-size
black-and-white picture of D.H. Lawrence on a publisher's advertising
poster and listened to Ornette Coleman's *This Is Our Music* for maybe
the tenth time in the Modern Times book and record shop at 2430 11th
Avenue in Regina, Saskatchewan. Near as I can reckon, that's when it

first occurred to me that I too might make a writer of myself. It was the winter of 1961 and I was sixteen verging on seventeen. Becoming a writer seemed to me a poor third choice to being able to play a saxophone like Ornette Coleman or becoming an artist with paint pots and a hundred pure bristle brushes who might bring more of D.H. Lawrence back to life with an oil portrait than that old photograph ever could, but writing was, as career counsellors are wont to say, 'a more viable option'. But what kind of writer? There were magazines, but serious people had stopped reading them seriously, all but *The New Yorker*. The new thing in people's lives was television and television needed writers, but television wasn't interesting to me, except occasionally, when I could see some of the music I loved being performed. Movies? I'd never thought about movies actually being written although I had heard about people who wrote scripts for movies. I knew about Senator Joseph McCarthy, HUAC, and Hollywood's blacklist. Hollywood was a dream factory. I wanted reality. I wanted the heightened reality of books. If I was to write, I wanted to write books that enriched the whole soul, emotional and mental. Imagine that! Writers of real books lived in London, like Mordecai Richler, and Paris like Mavis Gallant, and New York like Brian Moore. I did not want to live elsewhere than Canada even though I did want to live elsewhere in Canada, in Montreal, in Duddy Kravitz's Canada. Canada had made me and I was made for Canada, Canadian-built, stubborn with a low centre of gravity. The only person I knew who had the courage to even call herself a writer was Helene who co-owned Modern Times and was working on a poem at the front desk when I was standing and looking at D.H. Lawrence and reading Mordecai Richler and listening to Ornette Coleman in freedom and liberty and security. It was an afternoon when I'd skipped school and no questions were being asked of me except the questions I was asking of myself. It was a pretty good day. I was having a fairly good time.

Fast-forward nine years to another fairly good time in my life.

At twenty-five, after undergoing a religious conversion and studying to be a priest, after earning undergraduate degrees in philosophy and theology, after a loss of faith and an exit from the Catholic Church, after earning a graduate degree in world religions and falling in love and getting married, after writing my own stuff for at least an hour a day every day of those nine years, even after publishing a few things and starting a collection of rejection slips, I wanted to be a poet and now knew it was possible to be one in Canada. But I'd come to a great divide: what was to be done with the rest of my life? I had it on good authority, actually the best, because Irving Layton was arguably the best poet in English actually living in this country at the time, that if a poet worked past 9:30 a.m., he wasn't a real poet. A fiction writer, Layton figured, might reasonably sit at a desk until 1:00 p.m. Neither was steady work but both were as noble a calling as falling in love and into beds that were not your own. 'The problem is,' Layton said, 'that neither are worldly duties. Get a job that doesn't leave you grubbing for money. Even the Golden Boy has to write *songs* these days.' We – it was a university press conference not a solo interview – knew, without asking, who he meant by the Golden Boy. Leonard Cohen. If Leonard Cohen, poet and novelist, couldn't make a living from writing in Canada in the spring of 1969, what hope for prosperity was there for the likes of me?

I figured I might make a living as a copywriter in advertising.

'Just don't give up your liberty for security,' Layton roared.

If the grad student who shared an office with me in the religion department at McMaster hadn't encouraged me to offer my teaching services to a small college in Nova Scotia whose contract he'd just turned down, I might be very wealthy now and completely soul-destroyed from turning lumber patch buccaneers into smiling ever-friendly environmentalists with mere strokes of my pen. That's the best-paying fiction writing in the country. But I made the right call. I got an instructor's job in the religious studies department at Saint Mary's University that led to a short-term replacement contract at the University of Prince Edward Island that led to my present position at Dawson College. I became a long term multi-disciplinary junior college teacher. It beats running an elevator eight hours a day like Ornette Coleman once had to do. By a long chalk. It's secure. It's been liberating. I've taught a lot. I've learned a lot more. Seventeen- and eighteen-year-olds know more than how to simply look beautiful in each other's arms. They do know that but they also teach me to look for what they are too young to see – the beauty they don't yet possess. And they leave me enough free time to seek answers to a question that one day might interest them: Why is beauty such a rare thing?

Beauty, I teach, is a rare thing. Go for truth. It's easier to find but harder to hold. Be honest. Say what you see. Nothing else. Say it in your own voice, free of bullshit, raw or media-shaped. Shit happens. It piles up. In the long term, it turns to manure and does good. In the short term, it stinks. Believe what your nose tells you. In the long term, we're all dead.

I don't teach *creative writing*.

I'm not a *therapist*.

It's a fairly good job. I'm having a pretty good time.

'The first flash of fiction arrives without words. It consists of a fixed image, like a slide or (closer still) a freeze frame, showing characters in a simple situation,' writes Mavis Gallant. The end of this book came to me like that, as do the ends of all my books – fiction and non-fiction. Before I'd done more than sketch a rough outline of what *This Is Our Writing* was to be and do and how I'd incorporate the essays on Davies and Cohen already written, I knew that I was caught in a freeze frame in the kitchen of our flat on Grosvenor Avenue. I knew it was a Sunday night and I was at the sink scouring a pot or pan. And, it's mid-January 1997 and I'm almost ready to sink down into the living-room sofa in front of the final episode of Masterpiece Theater's *Nostromo* and unspin Joseph Conrad's fine web of moral complexity on the VCR in the company of Ann, my constant companion. Right now, at this instant, I'm messing about with two kinds of scouring pads and a big dollop of elbow grease in an effort to remove scorched pan drippings from the bottom of an enamelled roasting pan. I do my best thinking about the books I read and the books I write at home in our kitchen on a full stomach. I need a good home and good food to function well. It's an ordinary kitchen: there's a back window on to a neighbourhood rife with birds, squirrels, cats, dogs, people. Airplanes pass high overhead. Inside, there's a telephone, the daily newspaper filed in the recycling bag, the radio is tuned to CBC Stereo, some thoughts are being formulated.

The thought I'm thinking right now is this: whatever else you might want to say about my views of English-Canadian fiction writers and their books as a critic who's also a storyteller, you can't say they're vacuum-packed. I'm no more likely to read a book in a tower and massage it to a prickly stack of particles dribbling footnotes into a laptop than I'm ever likely to be found lunching on a tin of Campbell's soup. When we have to open a can of anything for quick sustenance in this house, it's Primo's Hearty Chicken Soup to which Ann or I have added some fresh broccoli, celery, carrots and oregano. We'll eat it with fresh baguette from the *boulangerie* around the corner and follow that with a bunch of Thompson grapes and a Granny Smith apple that's been peeled and cored and sliced into eighths with careful attention to equality. Get the picture?

I don't eat to live.

I don't live to eat.

I read for nourishment and avoid the quick fix of junk food whenever possible.

I live and eat and read a lot of things, some much better than others. I crave fibre and freshness and taste that ranges from pungent to subtle. Goodness too. In food. In books.

The bit of pork fat I'm trying to scour from the roasting pan is as problematic as Don Warner's syntax. I'm listening to *Jazz Land* from C B C Halifax with Don Warner. It has good music that pretty well speaks for itself but Don Warner insists on offering comments on the music that wouldn't be out of place at a Rotary Club luncheon alongside a microwave-drenched freshly unfrozen fillet of generic white fish. Warner's radiospeak is the kind of boosterism that doesn't do anybody's soul any good. He's rabbiting on about Charlie Haden's Quartet West, a group that's reviving the kind of West Coast jazz that made it into the Hollywood movies of the fifties, and he's saying this and he's saying that about Charlie Haden's illustrious career but he isn't alluding at all to Haden's jazz beginnings with Ornette Coleman. It strikes me with some force that not once, not ever, have I heard a single cut from *This Is Our Music* on his program. Not 'Blues Connotation' or 'Beauty Is a Rare Thing' or 'Kaleidoscope' or 'Embraceable You' or 'Poise' or 'Humpty Dumpty' or 'Folk Tale'.

I'm not saying Don Warner has never played them. I'm telling myself I've never heard him play them and I'm a regular listener so I'm betting you haven't heard them either even though these pieces and everything else Ornette Coleman recorded for Atlantic Records has been available on a boxed set titled *Beauty Is a Rare Thing* since 1993. Thank Rhino Records.

Does this matter?

Yes, this matters, even though it's 1999 now and Don Warner died earlier this year and *Jazz Land* was cancelled at the end of the 1997 season.

If I hadn't spent as much time as I did between 1958 and 1962, the years when I was in high school, listening to Ornette Coleman's music and following the arguments in *Down Beat* I might have more sympathy for the whines, whimpers and general sense of financial grievance and under-appreciation common among far too many English-Canadian fiction writers in and out of their books. Did you hear the Writers' Union of Canada's erstwhile president Susan Musgrave (who can be very funny) seriously propose *state pensions* for those writers of our generation who haven't provided for their own old age? Doesn't she know that nobody drafted us, we volunteered? But, ah then, Susan Musgrave is principally a poet and many poets are pleased to think that the word 'salary' is yet another example of esoteric jargon. As the American ex-poet Charles Baxter so nicely puts it in the issue of *Harper's* I was reading back in January 1997:

> Loyalty is a religion for poets, and in any case they need the requirements of friendship to fill the twenty-three and a half hours a day that they are not writing.

Maybe I'd be more willing to toe the CanLit party line in my criticisms of English-Canadian writing if *Down Beat* hadn't got me interested in the true stories of the people who made jazz. I've got more than musical reasons for being happy I listened to the music Ornette Coleman made on his white plastic alto saxophone with Don Cherry on pocket trumpet, Charlie Haden on bass, and Ed Blackwell or Billy Higgins on drums. Eavesdropping on the repercussive debate it generated has made me less comradely, less tribal in my loyalties but quickened my solidarity with something larger than self-absorption.

Yes, I did say *Don Cherry*. Nehmeh's dad, not the hockey guy. A *cool* dude, dead too soon.

Ornette Coleman's gig at New York's Five Spot café with his quartet in November 1959 had as decisive and divisive if not as pervasive an impact on American music as Bob Dylan's Newport Folk Festival appearance five years later. *This Is Our Music* was recorded on July 19th and August 2nd, 1960, while the jazz world divided into those who stood by Coleman and those who stood against him. There was no middle position.

I didn't know how to define Coleman's music but I knew it wasn't what most people meant by jazz in the Eisenhower era and Wynton Marsalis still means by that term most of the time he picks up his horn. I didn't care. I've never been much for labels outside grocery stores. When I tried to get one of my friends to listen to 'Blues Connotation', I told him Coleman's music was what rock and roll would sound like if the electric guitar hadn't been invented and it was played only by African musicians in a United States that had never known the peculiar institution of slavery. I had good, fast untrained ears then and I think I got it just about right even though my friend fled what he thought was bedlam in my bedroom and chatted up my older sister downstairs in my mother's kitchen instead. Ornette Coleman's music is the honest expression of a highly personal quest for beauty. It's truth seeking beauty. This is his truth as he expressed it in 1993 in a note attached to the *Beauty Is a Rare Thing* boxed set:

> Every person who has had a democratic experience by birth or by passport knows there are no hatreds or enemies in democracy, because everyone is an individual. Learning, doing, being, are the conversationship for perfecting, protecting, and caring of the belief existence as an individual in relationship to everyone, physically, mentally, spiritually – the concept of self.

So, of course – then being the USA, then being 1959 – nearly everybody told lies about Ornette Coleman, treated him dishonestly, dismissed him. When he said his music was *free jazz* a lot of people who ought to have known better said Ornette Coleman didn't know anything, was just *jiving*. They should have known better because it wasn't as if he was a brother from another planet. Ornette Coleman was twenty-nine when he played the Five Spot. He'd been playing professionally for a decade and had released three albums. But the thing was, he came out of Texas R&B bands via Louisiana-sanctified Spirit churches and had spent years of teaching himself classical music theory in Los Angeles while working as an elevator operator.

Can you imagine what it is to keep your mind alive in an elevator, eight hours a day?

Could you stand in his shoes? You can if you listen as *freely* as he played.

Coleman composed childlike melodies that crossed over into harmonies and harmonies that crossed over into melodies without conventional chord changes or keys, according to a structure he calls 'harmolodics' that is distinctly conceptual and profoundly systematic in its direct expression of thought and emotion and apparent sensory impressions. Ornette Coleman's goal was and is an art in which the feel of democracy comes through whatever the listener's emotional condition and intellectual presuppositions might be. Because of its raw blues inflections and group emphasis, some thought it was Afro-centric Black Power. Others, like the conductor Leonard Bernstein and the composer Gunther Schuller, looked at its complexity and saw it as a fusion of American and European classical, modernist and populist traditions into a new Third Stream. Those who thought he was *jiving* kept their fingers pointed right at Ornette Coleman's white plastic alto saxophone, Don Cherry's pocket trumpet and the Southern white teenager playing bass who had come into jazz from the Haden family's bluegrass band and guffawed. Me? I was just blown away by the Ornette Coleman Quartet's force, emphasis, excitement, pure ballsiness, voice.

Coleman's early music doesn't sound so strange now. For one thing, John Coltrane (who studied with Coleman) created a sonic bridge between Coleman and the bebop that had come before him. For another, unless you're blind in one ear and can't see out the other, it's obvious that Ornette Coleman broke with jazz conventions in just the same way as singers like Robert Johnson and Lightnin' Hopkins broke with work shouts, folk songs and church hymns by ignoring equal-tempered scales and using the micro-tones of West African pitch-tone languages where emotional intensity comes through flattening notes. It's just the *down home blues*, man. It's just a democratic human voice singing out – thoughts are free, no scholar can map them, no huntsman can trap them, *die Gedanken sind frei.*

What's with the German? Germans don't get the blues, do they?

They do if they're born under the wrong Tsar in Russia before the Revolution.

They do if they start life in Canada in a sod hut.

They do if they farm dirt in the Great Depression.

They do if all their relatives who stayed back in the USSR were declared enemies of the state and exiled to the Gulag by Uncle Joe Stalin simply for being able to speak German.

My grandparents and parents lived the blues on the Great Canadian Plains.

I'm a democrat by birth not passport. For me, the blues are formative not normative. I was born in liberty and security with a prospect of prosperity. I was born in Saskatchewan during the final weeks of the campaign that brought the first socialist government in North America to power. The man who lived next door to my father's house was a Baptist preacher. He taught me to recite the freedom-seeking poetry of Robert Burns as I learned to speak. He taught me about the ways of powerful people. He was a fine storyteller. He was also a working politician and the premier of the province. He was the Reverend T.C. Douglas. Tommy Douglas had a pithy expressiveness and could take the piss out of anyone. He knew better than most how much we'd been victimized by banks and railroads: he taught some of us who needed the lesson that none of us were victims.

Never live half a life when a whole life is available.

Nobody owns you until you sell yourself short.

It never ceases to amaze me, how readily and easily so many English Canadians do both. Writers included. We were born in liberty and security with a prospect of prosperity. Or picked that up with our passports. And yet the Margaret Atwood of *Survival* attracted a huge following by portraying middle-class Canadian women as *victims* of lousy sex with dysfunctional dickheads. Right. Think about Thelonius Monk hating the sound of his own best tune because every time it was played he was being robbed of his royalties. Think about Miles Davis and his beatings by cops who didn't like the guy because he was talented enough to own Italian sports cars and bop white chicks who freely chose to join their beauty and passion to his. Think about Charles Mingus having to pose as a Latin American when he played with Red Norvo in order to share the same stage: Mingus called his autobiography *Beneath the Belly of the Underdog*. And these are *success* stories in the jazz world. I won't mention Billie Holiday or Bessie Smith – they'd have whopped the 'do off the head of any ofay chick called them *victims*. Think about the Canadian jazzers whose stories Mark Miller tells in *Jazz in Canada: 14 Lives* (1982) and *Boogie, Pete and the Senator* (1987). Mark Miller interviewed the drummer Larry Dubin and Dubin confessed, 'I just wanted to be a jazz musician. But more than even wanting to be a jazz musician, I wanted to be the musician I wanted to be.' And I think about the musicians who would crowd a corner of Modern Times in duos or trios or quartets after Kerry and Helene, the co-owners, had rolled the moveable bookshelves out of the way, and play for three or four hours on a mid-week night for maybe ten or twenty people like me who liked what they did. And they played for the sheer mad celebratory freedom and joy of it and maybe a case of beer.

The controversy that swirled around Ornette Coleman drew me deeper into jazz and black culture. I'd listened to Miles Davis. Now I listened to Charles Mingus. From Charles Mingus, I picked up references to Duke Ellington and checked him out. Ah, Duke and his orchestra, his only duchess. Read Duke's *Music Is My Mistress*. Irving Mills did what the New York Mob wanted and retained the services of the Duke Ellington Sextet for Harlem's Cotton Club in 1928. The band doubled in size and with increased size came extraordinary musical strength: Duke Ellington hired players from every significant African-American community from Chicago to New Orleans, Boston to Houston to the Caribbean, so that his orchestra could speak all the dialects of black experience even if they were stuck up in Harlem playing to 'White Only' audiences. And the Duke Ellington Orchestra's shows at the Cotton Club became concerts of brilliantly executed original music and the Duke became a *maestro*. Among other things, he invented the jazz ballad. 'Mood Indigo.' Irving Mills collected 50 per cent of composer's royalties on every piece Duke wrote and 100 per cent of the publisher's royalties plus management fees on every public appearance and record deal. That wasn't fair. That wasn't right. But Duke Ellington would never say a word against Irving Mills. There was something more important involved than money: security, liberty, artistry. Irving Mills insisted that the Duke Ellington Orchestra was treated with the respect due the living instrument of America's foremost composer. Try to *victimize* Duke Ellington and Irving Mills would turn Rottweiler on you.

In comparison with the dolphin-like jazzmen whose music floats over shark-infested waters, far too many English-Canadian fiction writers seem to form a shoal of whitings hugging too safe a shore, spawn of

Northrop Frye's mythic visions that find sustenance in mutual admiration and Canada Council writing grants. I find them naive, terribly naive.

You don't need an advanced degree in economics to know that nobody ever made a good living strictly out of writing non-genre novels in this century unless they flattered and encouraged tribal loyalties. The novelists who pop into your head who are exceptions to the dismal rule that fiction doesn't pay as well as dentistry worked in their day for American mass-circulation magazines when those magazines paid as much for a single story as a college teacher then earned in a year. Scott Fitzgerald. Ernest Hemingway. William Faulkner. We can thank *The New Yorker* a little and her own modest appetites a lot more that Mavis Gallant has *lived* purely on her fictions. Others have had to write for newspapers. Or write for the movies. Or, more recently, write for extremely glossy magazines and newspapers and for film studios and select books for the Book-of-the-Month Club and still lust after the incomes of better paid orthodontists. Mordecai Richler.

Tiring of the abuse of his critics, Ornette Coleman wanted to become a full-time teacher, craved his own college of music, went so far as to buy an abandoned school but never made enough money from his music to open it. He sold that building a couple of years ago to a real estate developer for several million dollars.

Go for truth and sometimes you hit a beautiful jackpot you didn't know was out there.

Out here, in my kitchen in the winter of 1997, I'm wearing a black T-shirt. The logo on the front says *nobody owns us.* Some of the people I work out with at the Westmount Y M C A want to buy it off my back. I won't sell it. I didn't buy it. It came to me in the mail – free. Not quite. Like a few dozen other people, I donate ten dollars to *This Magazine* every month to help them pay their office rent. *Wear your politics on your sleeve* it says on the left sleeve. That's good advice: it keeps you from letting politics buy space inside your head that ought to be given up only to beauty. Beauty is a rare thing.

Here. Now.

Tomorrow, for dinner, Ann and I will have leftover cold pork tenderloin slices flavoured with *moutarde Dijon et fines herbes,* red cabbage with onions and apples in a red wine vinegar and caraway dressing. Leftovers.

We don't eat to live.

We don't live to eat.

We read for nourishment and avoid the quick fix of junk food whenever possible.

I live and eat and read a lot of things, some much better than others. I crave fibre and freshness and a range of taste from hot to cold, pungent to subtle. Goodness, yes.

I do my best thinking about books at home in our kitchen on a full stomach.

On this night in January 1997, it takes fifteen minutes to scour the roasting pan and think this essay through. It will take me six weeks to write a first draft, writing for an hour a day. I can't spare more time. In those six weeks, I'll have people to see, places to go, things to do that I think of as complements to my writing, not distractions: writing is what you do in the time you're not doing other things. As those six weeks unwind, I'll

– do a final edit of my novel *Badass on a Softail* for autumn publication
– begin teaching some students to closely observe social behaviour in a structured way
– get some other students to consider whether Chappie, the protagonist of Russell Banks's *Rule of the Bone,* is evil, stupid, a victim of unfortunate circumstances or something else.
– shovel a lot of snow
– listen to Grigory Sokolov play Rachmaninov as a soloist with the Montreal Symphony Orchestra
– listen to the Montreal Symphony play Stravinsky and Dvorak
– hear the Emerson Quartet play Schubert and Brahms
– read several books on the origins of Christianity and its early stages of development in Europe
– research a spate of recent apparitions of the Blessed Virgin Mary and comment upon the Virgin of the Seminole Insurance Building of Clearwater, Florida, on a local morning television chat-show
– go to the movies and see *Touch* and think about Elmore Leonard's satirical view of American religion and compare the movie version to the original book for my own benefit before talking about the movie, more simply, on local morning television

– keep muscle tone up and weight down working out in the weight room of the Westmount Y M C A a couple of times every week

– reread several books by Hugh Hood

When a journalist asked Leonard Cohen what exactly was he doing in the *zendo* on Mount Baldy where he was then spending a lot of his time, he replied, 'Making the best fucking soup in the world.'

That's my kind of answer. You crave spiritual illumination, you need reflective experiences, you go to where the heat is, you start cooking in the kitchen. Or whatever room you call your own.

That's why I'm listening to Ornette Coleman's 'Embraceable You' as I write this sentence. Here. Now. And tomorrow, I'll start two new books – one as a reader, another as a writer. I hope they'll cook – without gas. Books written by writers who can truthfully say, 'I just wanted to be a writer. But more than even wanting to be a writer, I wanted to be the writer I wanted to be.'

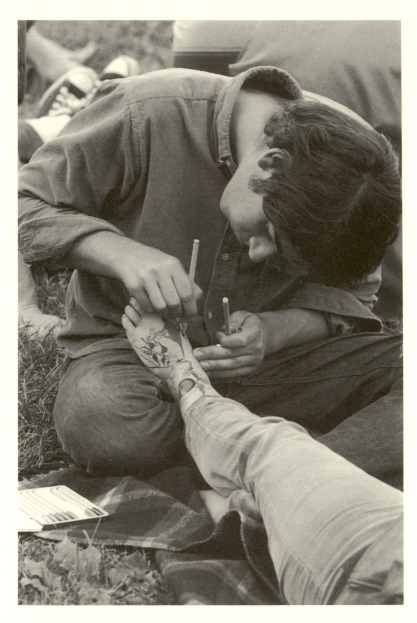

Love-in, Fletcher's Fields, 1967

Why Read What They Write?

In the November 1, 1983, issue of the *Financial Post Magazine* there's an article by Marjorie Harris titled 'You Don't Have to Read Canadian: Our Namedropper's Guide Will Do' that's funny in both intended and unintended ways and still worth a second look at this further distance. I don't know who Marjorie Harris was then and assume she's now the popular gardening journalist by that name, but I do know enough about the *Financial Post Magazine* to conclude that it must have found CanLit fashionable and financially interesting in 1983 or this article would not have been printed. After stating a few rules of thumb such as 'Take note of foreign acclaim. We regard our literary stars seriously only when they've been recognized outside the country,' she addresses the question 'Who is on the bus?'

> The *Who's Who* of Canadian literature is a finite entity that has been likened to a bus. There are only so many seats available. When a new person gets on, someone else gets tossed off. A publishing explosion took place in the mid- to late '60s, and the publishing industry believes that we started reading more indigenous works per capita than they do in the United States. But the size of the bus remained the same in terms of who could be In or Out.

Harris lists the following as 'In' *with tenure* – Morley Callaghan, Hugh MacLennan, W.O. Mitchell, Robertson Davies – and these 'In' *with foreign acclaim* – Mordecai Richler, Robertson Davies (again), Margaret Laurence, Alice Munro, Margaret Atwood – and these simply 'In' – Dave Godfrey, Hugh Hood, W.D. Valgardson, Clark Blaise, Matt Cohen, Alden Nowlan – and these 'In' but manoeuvring for position – Michael Ondaatje, Jack Hodgins, Carol Shields, Leon Rooke, Susan Musgrave. The 'Outs' you have to guess for yourself. It's fair to conclude, though, that Harris is smart enough to place Mavis Gallant in a separate category that's 'above' the others and more 'neglected' by these assertions:

Most Neglected Fine Novel – Mavis Gallant's *Green Water, Green Sky*
Best Volume of Short Stories Not by Mavis Gallant – either Alice
Munro's *Dance of the Happy Shades* or *Jupiter's Moon* (sic)

Harris extends her lists with the following:

Most Impenetrable Novel – Dave Godfrey's *The New Ancestors*
Most Neglected Novel of Ideas – Sara Jeannette Duncan's *The Imperial-
ist*
Best Volume of Canadian Short Stories Not by a Canadian –
Malcolm Lowry's *Hear Us O Lord from Heaven Thy Dwelling Place,
Dark Is the Grave Wherein My Friend Is Laid*
Most Ambitious Novelist – Hugh Hood
Most Schizophrenic Historical Novel – John Richardson's *Wacousta*
Most Coherent Historical Novel – Timothy Findley's *The Wars*
Most Overrated (Or Underrated) Novel in CanLit –
Margaret Laurence's *The Diviners*
Most American Canadian Novel – Leonard Cohen's *Beautiful Losers*
Best Novel of Immigrant Experience – Adele Wiseman's *The Sacrifice*
Most Prolific Canadian Writer – Margaret Atwood

When Marjorie Harris turns to literary criticism and some other genres,
she notes that Canada has Northrop Frye as our only critic but he's 'a
giant' and that William French is the 'dean of Canadian reviewers' but
has no assistants of any calibre: she deplores book review sections of
daily newspapers as hack-ridden. Under the heading 'Comic Relief', she
writes, 'The impression you get at literary bashes is that we are not a bar-
relful of laughs. Untrue.' She cites Mordecai Richler's *Cocksure*, Jack
McLeod's *Zinger And Me*, John Metcalf's *General Ludd* and *Kicking
Against the Pricks*, Marian Engel's *Lunatic Villas*, Morley Torgov's *A
Good Place to Come From*, Robert Kroetsch's *Studhorse Man*, and
anoints Edward O. Phillips' *Sunday's Child* as 'best' of all. Her list of
Canadian crime-fiction writers includes John Reeves, Howard Engel,
Tim Wynne-Jones, L.A. Morse, Sara Woods and 'newcomer' Eric
Wright.

In the penultimate paragraph of her article, Marjorie Harris mentions 'The Glenn Ford/Yvonne De Carlo Syndrome' – 'the contentious

issue of who is, and who isn't, a Canadian writer.' The problem cases are Malcolm Lowry, Saul Bellow and Brian Moore:

> But Brian Moore (1921–) tops the list. He's one of the great novelists of this century and any country would gladly scoop him up. But can we? He was born in Ireland, lived in Canada long enough to acquire a passport and write *The Luck of Ginger Coffey*, then moved swiftly to Malibu, Calif. He returns regularly to collect awards, be a writer-in-residence and see his buddies.

Writers she refers to *en passant* include Graeme Gibson (as Atwood's 'co-vivant', as novelist, and as ex-husband of Shirley Gibson, whose name is dropped in alongside those of Dennis Lee and James Polk as the brains and brawn of House of Anansi) and Kildare Dobbs and Richard Wright (as novelists who are 'buddies' of Brian Moore).

Sixteen years later, there really is such a guidebook as *Who's Who in Canadian Literature*. It's published by Reference Press and the 1997–98 edition lists over a thousand writers, English and French. Has Marjorie Harris's magic bus become a double-decker commuter train with writers stacked on top of one another? Or is it more like a jumbo jet with connections to a lot of foreign destinations? Anyone who follows the action of foreign rights sales through the 'In the Works' column of *Quill & Quire* knows that quite a number of 'our literary stars' are far better recognized in England, Denmark, Germany, France, Italy and Japan than they are at home – Barbara Gowdy or Steven Heighton, for instance. The questions now seem to be, who's in First, who gets Business, why is Tourist overbooked and can there really be that many on Standby? Who among us in all our variety understands Brian Moore's old-fashioned idea – 'that there should be a company of the good' among writers that is bound together by aesthetics not six-figure advances?

I dredged Marjorie Harris's article up from an old file folder some months ago, after a casual conversation with my colleague Sally Todd Nelson provided an unintended *aide memoire*. Sally is an influential teacher who's known for a number of things, including her discovery of David Fennario in one of our Dawson College classrooms and encouraging his talent by starting up Dawson College Press and publishing

Without a Parachute, the book that opened doors at Centaur Theatre for his plays. A nice move. Sally also organized an extensive series of readings by English-Canadian authors that lasted years and years and put a lot of Quebec college students into direct contact with writers from the rest of Canada for the first time. Sally and I were casually talking of many things (including the recent death of Brian Moore on January 11, 1999) when she mentioned that she'd given up organizing those reading series in the mid-eighties when she realized that she just couldn't keep up with the rapid expansion in English-Canadian writing any longer and figure out for herself who was hot and who was not. All the while we talked, I kept noticing the copy of Joyce's *A Portrait of the Artist as a Young Man* she was carrying: it was wonderfully well-thumbed! As well-thumbed as Brian Moore's own copy must have been, I imagined. A couple of hours later, neither Joyce nor Ireland nor Moore entirely out of mind, I remembered Marjorie Harris's article and my reasons for keeping it on file all these years.

In November 1983 when 'You Don't Have to Read Canadian' was printed, my first novel was six months old and I was trying my hand at some literary journalism of my own. A 'Books' column of mine in the *Montreal Review* had ended with the collapse of that magazine the previous year and I was trying to freelance various things. So I started making notes for a piece called 'You Don't Have to Read Atwood and Her Cadre to Read Canadian Fiction' that was an answer to Marjorie Harris who'd mentioned Atwood more times than I thought she merited in her own right (Most Prolific Canadian Writer? Scarcely that, when the competition was Robin Skelton, George Woodcock and George Bowering and even that left aside W.E. Dan Ross of Saint John long before he tallied out with a total of 314 titles to his credit in 1995). Harris also used the term 'Atwood Generation' to cover all the writers who had emerged in the late sixties, even Hugh Hood who was born before Mordecai Richler! My notes went in two directions: I wanted to establish the fact that there was a larger community of English-Canadian writers worth reading who predated the era of Atwood (including Hugh Hood) and that the post-war baby boom was in the middle of producing a wave of good new writing in Canada that Harris overlooked entirely and that I predicted would soon eclipse the work of Atwood and associates in everything except the publicity and self-regard so eagerly sought and found by Canadian equivalents of the 'shameless little puffers-up of their talents and muggers-in-public for anyone who would write them up' who had caused Brian Moore to flee the New York literary world in disgust. I noted some writers of achievement not on the Harris bus – Norman Levine, Jack Ludwig, Rudy Wiebe, Jane Rule, Leon Rooke, George McWhirter, Barry Callaghan, Alistair Macleod, Kent Thompson, David Helwig, Tom Marshall, Ray Smith, Audrey Thomas. Noting that Harris excluded nature writers, I jotted down the names of two very good ones – Roderick Haig-Brown and R.D. Symons. Then I started a list of writers and books that came my way between '77 and '83 that sketched rough contours of the coming Boom!

Edna Alford, *A Sleep Full of Dreams* (1981)

Byrna Barclay, *Summer of the Hungry Pup* (1981)

Sandra Birdsell, *Night Travellers* (1982)

Ann Copeland, *At Peace* (1978)

Brian Fawcett, *My Career with the Leafs* (1982)

Keath Fraser, *Taking Cover* (1982)

Douglas Glover, *The Mad River* (1981)

Greg Hollingshead, *Famous Players* (1982)

Janette Turner Hospital, *The Ivory Swing* (1982)

M.T. Kelly, *I Do Remember the Fall* (1977), *The Ruined Season* (1982)

Joy Kogawa, *Obasan* (1983)

Jake MacDonald, *Indian River* (1981)

David McFadden, *A Trip Around Lake Erie* (1980),
    A Trip Around Lake Huron (1980)

Veronica Ross, *Goodbye Summer* (1980)

John Ralston Saul, *The Birds of Prey* (1977), *Baraka* (1983)

Bill Schermbrucker, *Chameleon* (1983)

J.J. Steinfeld, *The Apostate's Tattoo* (1983)

Merna Summers, *Calling Home* (1982)

Susan Swan, *The Biggest Modern Woman of the World* (1983)

George Szanto, *Not Working* (1983)

Aritha van Herk, *The Tent Peg* (1981)

Guy Vanderhaeghe, *Man Descending* (1982)

It's tempting to be a revisionist, to go back and fill in what I missed completely in those years and excise some things that now seem less sparkling and more puffed-up than at first sight. But those are the writers who caught my attention with these books in that time through the precision of their descriptions of the world, their accumulation of telling detail, their wide-ranging attempts to capture contemporary consciousness and their travels within uncharted parts of the human world.

Some of these writers and any number of others whose books were published in the next five years first came into my view through Canadian literary magazines that were 'as obscure as their contributors' as Brian Moore described them in *The Mangan Inheritance* (1979), one of my favourite novels of that period. Was it my desire to know more of the Jamie Mangans who 'contribute' to that world or was it a more opaque sense that I was more likely to find Moore's 'company of the good' among their pages than elsewhere that set me to reading *Waves, Matrix, Descant* and, above all, *Canadian Fiction Magazine?* These were the ones that I bought, read and pressed into the hands of less regularly employed writers I knew, as I started to discover, in the mixture of things they offered, some good writing. By which I mean writing that was more focused on the conscious lives of contemporary people and less on massaging tribal Celtic signs, symbols and types of 'culture' (which Moore sends up, via the Mangans) into pleasing patterns upon which careers could be made in the manner of Robertson Davies, Timothy Findley, Margaret Atwood and their acolytes.

By 1982, *Canadian Fiction Magazine* had become successor to the *Tamarack Review* as *the* place to be published if you were any good because it published the best of the good. Nowadays, I wish I'd accumulated a complete collection of *Canadian Fiction Magazine*. Even more, I wish a cumulative index to *Canadian Fiction Magazine* existed: some university in southern Ontario ought to purchase its archive and install Geoff Hancock in an office somewhere and set him to work writing a definitive study of the emergence of the boomers in Canadian writing of the late seventies and eighties. Here's part of what Hancock (who edited four issues a year of *Canadian Fiction Magazine* between 1976 and 1997) writes in 'The Achievement of Canadian Fiction' – his introduction to *The Silver Anniversary Anthology of Canadian Fiction Magazine* (1997):

CFM has published social realism, symbol-based and image-based fiction, great slabs of the imagination that slice and whack away at the institutional conventions of fiction. Extra-literary problems became the event of the story, once called a fiction, now called a text. The story of our origins. A society in innocence. Our spiritual growth. Our terrible dramas. Our fecund imagination. Our soul's residence in darkness.

Stories published in CFM presented new models of perception. In the grey time of Canada, we answered the question posed by Northrop Frye: *where is here?* Canada doesn't exist except as a name we give to an abstract idea, best seen in our art and our fictions. Stories published in CFM have placed special emphasis on a new way to see. Stories in CFM might use a deconstruction model: plot replaced by ongoing incident; characters replaced by consciousness struggling with circumstance; social realism replaced by a sense of situation; form not *about* experience, but *more* experience so that fiction became a record of its own making.

Stories in CFM have used high culture and pop; been avant garde and generic, been comprised of parodies and intertexts; have challenged traditional concepts of character with anti-characters, and marginalized viewpoints. CFM authors have expressed a wide variety of styles, subjects, forms, contents. In the maturing of our nation's fiction, CFM has challenged the conventional definition of the classic short story which consisted of a neat triad of qualities: making a single impression on a reader, concentrating on a crisis, and making the crisis pivotal in a controlled plot.

Under Hancock's editorship, CFM published over one thousand stories. Each year for twenty years, a Contributor's Prize was given to the best story of the year: the winning writers include Leon Rooke, W.P. Kinsella, Mavis Gallant, John Metcalf, Guy Vanderhaeghe, Keath Fraser, David Sharpe, Douglas Glover, Patrick Roscoe, Matt Cohen, Ann Copeland, Rohinton Mistry, Frances Itani, Sharon Butala, Chetan Rejani, T.F. Rigelhof, Barbara Gowdy, Greg Stephenson, Susan Crawford, Thomas Wharton. That's why I call what happened a Boom!

It's always difficult to sort out the effects of any explosion but Oberon

Press has made a more consistent and valiant attempt than I ever did. Through the annual series now known as *Coming Attractions* that first began life in 1980 under the title *First Impressions* and the editorship of John Metcalf and is now edited by Maggie Helwig, three good new writers are featured every year. Here is the sequence of writers of promise Oberon editors discovered in the obscure land of literary magazines:

1980	Martin Avery	Isabel Huggan	Mike Mason
1981	Peter Behrens	Linda Svendsen	Ernest Hekkanen
1982	Barry Dempster	Don Dickinson	Dave Margoshes
1983	Sharon Butala	Bonnie Burnard	Sharon Sparling
1984	Diane Schoemperlen	Joan Fern Shaw	Michael Rawdon
1985	Sheila Delany	Francis Itani	Judith Pond
1986	Dayv James-French	Lesley Krueger	Rohinton Mistry
1987	Charles Foran	Patricia Bradbury	Cynthia Holz
1988	Christopher Fisher	Carol Anne Wien	Rick Hillis
1989	Brian Burke	Michelle Heinemann	Jean Rysstad
1990	Peter Stockland	Sara McDonald	Steven Heighton
1991	Ellen McKeough	Robert Majzels	Patricia Seaman
1992	Caroline Adderson	Marilyn Eisenstat	Marina Endicott
1993	Gayla Reid	Hannah Grant	Barbara Parkin
1994	Donald McNeill	Elise Levine	Lisa Moore
1995	Warren Cariou	Marilyn Gear Pilling	François Bonneville
1996	Lewis DeSoto	Murray Logan	Kelley Aitken
1997	Elyse Gasco	Dennis Bock	Nadine McInnis
1998	Leona Theis	Gabriella Goliger	Daryl Whetter

Through most of the nineties I've relied on *Coming Attractions* to point out new writers who might to be included in a company of the good writers in this country. I've depended upon it in a way that wasn't necessary a decade earlier for the simple reason that I've pretty much given up reading Canadian literary magazines 'obscure as their contributors'. A large part of my reason for not reading them is that in 1989 McClelland & Stewart launched *The Journey Prize Anthology* with an endowment from James Michener's donation of all Canadian royalties of his 1988 novel *Journey.*

Each year for the past ten, *The Journey Prize Anthology* has printed a dozen or so stories from a stack that have been pre-selected as 'the best' by the literary journals that first published them. One story is awarded $10,000 and a further $2,000 goes to the journal that published it. If you can get 'the best' in one-stop shopping, why bother with the rest? That's just a partial answer: Oberon's longer-lived annual *Best Canadian Stories* never used to keep me from little magazines. The difference? The Oberon collection always offers one or two (at most) editorial points of view – with all the quirkiness and possibilities for spirited argument that involves – whereas the *Journey* anthology seems to be largely the work of an M&s editorial committee adjudicating decisions made earlier by editorial committees at the literary mags, with money and prestige (which brings more money in the form of larger arts grants) hanging in the balance. Whatever else that is, it's not a recipe for challenging readers and critics in their prejudices about what is or is not important. Another part of my avoidance of the literary mags is that CBC Radio in combination with a changing sponsorship has been running a literary competition simultaneously with the Journey Prize that really ought to be called 'The Robert Weaver Awards' (in honour of the CBC producer and former editor of the *Tamarack Review* who has never read a story about a young person serendipitously encountering an older person and discovering an unspoken truth that he didn't like) with the same kind of prize money and publication in *Saturday Night*. Taken together, this means that a lot of short fiction in this country is first written for submission to the CBC. Then, after it's been rejected there, it's submitted to whichever journal has the best record for getting things selected by the Journey committee. If it doesn't make it there, it goes on to the second from the top journal *und so weiter*. At the journals themselves, selections tend more and more to be made exclusively by editorial committees who have much to gain if one of their selections gets chosen by the Journey committee. Moore's idea – 'that there should be a company of the good' – has devolved in Canada at the fag end of this century among the now-less-obscure contributors to the now-more-obscure Canadian literary magazines into a notion that there should be a company of technically proficient short fiction wordsmiths banging out nice little niches into which to slot politically correct jewel-like stories suitable for CBC and Journey selections.

It's easy enough to understand how it happened: few literary

magazines in this country have fiction editors with the guts and gump-
tion to articulate editorial policies and standards in each issue like Geoff
Hancock had always done with CFM, and even fewer have the chutzpah
and energy to select stories autocratically after reading and judging
every submission individually. Every little magazine is swamped with
hundreds of submissions of all sorts for every issue and almost every one
of them has responded with assembly-line adjudication. Adjudication
of what? Of cookie-cutter prose, ever so cautiously baked in the
workshop of university-sponsored creative writing classes? If you want
to be a literary writer, why not spend a semester or even two working on
a single short story or even half a dozen with the same kind of nutty
obsessiveness that Princess Di devoted to her colon's irrigation, when
the rewards are credits towards a degree in the short term, short-listing
for a big prize or even (be still my beating heart!) the prize itself in the
medium term, and the likelihood of a publishing contract with a decent
advance in the long term? Or am I being cynical? Not half so cynical as
the wilting if not withered writers who accept cheap wages to award easy
credits towards lazy degrees to those who are willing to learn how to
write the kinds of stories that have been winning the prizes. The final
result, to this reader's eye (whether I'm accurate or wildly misinformed
as to the causes), is less risk-taking all around, high degrees of technical
competence, the kind of unthinking un-prejudice usually labelled political correctness even though there's rarely anything political in it, and
ever more stories that are rapidly becoming as *therapeutic* as Canadian
poetry. I don't know if Alberto Manguel is right to praise Richard
Outram's poems quite as extravagantly as he does (oh blessed fault!) in
Into the Looking-Glass Wood (1998) but he's dead-on when he takes on
Canadian poetry as defined by Margaret Atwood in her selections for
the 1982 Oxford anthology, the standard against which too many have
been measuring themselves too bloody long:

> ... the style of what became recognized as Canadian poetry was
> simple-sounding, chatty, intimate though never overwhelmingly
> passionate, well-mannered though sometimes effectively ironic,
> often funny, in obligatory free verse.... It is as if, in the long
> beginning, Canadian literature chose to be easy ...

As a reader, I know I haven't lost my edge any more than Alberto Manguel but it's an open question whether either the CBC or Journey juries would know what to do with a strop and a straight razor if they were ever handed them.

If there's an upside to the literary largesse of the CBC's alliance with *Saturday Night* and M&S's use of the Michener fund, it's that some passionate and some memorable stories (K.D. Miller's, Mary Borsky's, Elyse Gasco's and Dennis Bock's spring immediately to mind as being so fully realized not even a confederacy of dunces could overlook them) that are notable for intensity of feeling, thickness of texture and lushness of detail have been brought to wider attention. And the Journey and CBC prizes do seem to have accelerated the development of a few good writers (even some who are survivors of creative writing bake-ups) and lifted them out of obscurity. We do need *speed*: it takes too damn long to break from the pack and establish yourself as a distinct presence in our literature. When Diane Schoemperlen won the Governor General's Award for Fiction in 1998 for *Forms of Devotion*, fourteen years and seven books after she was one of 1984's *Coming Attractions*, far too many people – including some in the media – asked 'Who she?' instead of the more appropriate, 'Has the student finally surpassed her master?' Like a lot of other writers of the past quarter century, Diane Schoemperlen cribbed from Alice Munro's early work: unlike most of the rest, Schoemperlen took not just subject matter but precision of language and innovation of form from Munro and has moved into regions of the heart, head and art that are distinctly her own.

From a bystander's point of view, it's always interesting and sometimes diverting to watch such writers as Diane Schoemperlen and Rohinton Mistry blossom, flower and mature to full stature. But it's also been depressing to see how long it takes even the most ambitious of those writers who hold firmly to Moore's idea of 'a company of the good' to make any kind of impact with a larger reading public. During the past twenty years, there have been occasional exceptions, writers like Guy Vanderhaeghe who exploded out of magazines 'as obscure as their contributors' and into his first book in 1982 and a Governor General's Award for it in 1983 and has never been out of the public eye, thanks to his fans Douglas Gibson at McClelland & Stewart and Peter Gzowski at *Morningside*. More often than not, it takes ten or more years of solid work to become eligible for even more limited 'overnight success.' And lasting success? A lot are still counting on posterity.

When the Journey Prize was first announced, some writers and editors optimistically expected that the result would be much wider attention being paid to the couple of dozen gifted fiction writers who had been working for years in the shadows of Gallant, Munro, Hood, Blaise and Metcalf without gaining much recognition beyond minuscule coteries. So it was a pleasure, not a surprise, to see Anne Copeland and M.G. Vassanji appear in the first year of the Journey anthology, Douglas Glover, Terry Griggs, Cynthia Flood and Wayne Tefs the next. What nobody I know expected was that so many new contributors would appear so soon and so few of either the old or the new would make repeat appearances. If I've done my sums correctly, the Journey anthologies have published 128 stories by 112 different writers in the ten years of its existence: sixty-five different women have contributed seventy-two stories, nine contributors have made two appearances, K.D. Miller has appeared three times and David Bergen holds the record at four appearances. Of the 112, a mere eleven have also been featured among Oberon's 'Coming Attractions' (Francis Itani, Steven Heighton, Dayv James-French, Jean Rysstad, Caroline Adderson, Marina Endicott, Gayla Reid, Elise Levine, Elyse Gasco, Dennis Bock, Gabriella Goliger). Steven Heighton and Gabriella Goliger are the only two who have had more than one story in Journey and been made a Coming Attraction. Steven Heighton is also one of ten Journey contributors who have gone on to publish books with Porcupine's Quill.

Heighton's achievements are worth looking at in more detail: he's a good writer in ways that any fan of Brian Moore will appreciate. The resemblances between them go beyond a desire to render the real world with precision. Both are meditative writers, writers who carefully explore and claim what Moore called 'emotional territories' and travel imaginatively between them in ways that make the foreign familiar and the familiar foreign.

In the June 10, 1995, *Globe and Mail*, Geraldine Sherman wrote:

The publication history behind Kingston, Ont., writer Steven Heighton's new collection provides a painful lesson in the isolation of the short-story writer. Ten of the eleven stories have appeared before, most of them several times, in different forms, always in literary journals such as *Matrix, Geist* and *Exile*. Many specialized periodicals have readerships so small and finances so precarious that would-be writers are required to buy subscriptions before editors will even read their manuscripts. With fees low or non-existent, a 'successful' writer can often lose money getting printed. While half a dozen lucrative prizes dangle like carrots before legions of writers, most practitioners rely on grants and the hope that a book publisher will eventually reprint their stories. In 1992, Heighton's first collection appeared, *Flight Paths of the Emperor* – fourteen marvellous stories, including several that had won prizes, all of them linked by the author's experience teaching English in Japan. That book sold 1,600 copies. With the help of five federal and provincial funding agencies, the same publisher, The Porcupine's Quill, of Erin, Ont., has now produced *On Earth As It Is*. It contains echoes of the large talent demonstrated in his earlier work....

On March 27th, 1993, Sherman had previously written of *Flight Paths of the Emperor*:

If one aim of the Trillium competition is to focus attention on work that might otherwise have slipped through the critical net, we must be grateful for the occasion to assess Heighton's marvellously intelligent first collection of stories, *Flight Paths of the Emperor*. Several stories have already been singled out for awards and reproduced in literary anthologies. But it's only now, with Heighton's work gathered in a single volume, that we can appreciate the extent of his talent, even as we become aware of his weakness. Most of Heighton's stories revolve around Japan, a country that has obviously captured his imagination. In a dozen different ways, he tries to show how one particular place and not another enters a person's consciousness and transforms his life. The narrator who appears in several stories is a young man very like the author, a teacher of English for a year in Osaka and a sympathetic student of Japanese life and language.... Often the stories begin with a Japanese proverb or a quote from a Japanese newspaper, a few lines that set the mind flying. For instance, from an ad for the Clean Cemetery Company that appeared in *The Japan Times*, December 10, 1987: 'From now on, Japanese who are too busy or live too far from family grave sites can pay to have professionals visit and clean the graves and burn incense in their place.'... In Heighton's work, travel propels the imagination homeward and provides fresh insight into familiar experience. He begins in one place and time, then moves back and forth across continents and generations. In this collection, one becomes aware of the excessive use of this technique. Too many objects or events are endowed with the attributes of Proust's madeleine, the power to shape memory. Occasionally the narrative breaks under the strain of forced connections. Still, each story is beautifully told, the language always precise, reflecting Heighton's past as a poet and his current role as editor of the Kingston literary magazine, *Quarry*. In many ways he's like the young Ondaatje, also a poet and editor, a superb craftsman at ease in foreign places and distant times, a sympathetic and watchful traveller able to sift through scattered experiences until they acquire meaning.

Geraldine Sherman praises the right things in Heighton's stories but is more irritated than she ought to be by what she finds excessive in his techniques. Encountering Steven Heighton in 1990, I too was reminded of the young Ondaatje. Heighton's first poetry book, *Stalin's Carnival*, had just won the Gerald Lampert Award and it was as stylish as he was when our paths crossed in Kingston at the annual general meeting of the Writers' Union of Canada: Heighton's hair was long and curly, he wore a black leather motorcycle jacket with panache and had the verbal moves of the kind of guitar-slinging poet a lot of undergraduates like to look at, listen to and take to bed as a book. On attitude alone, Heighton looked like he'd have no difficulty breaking through to a sizeable audience very quickly. But he had more going for him than pop idol good looks and iconic style: even in casual conversation, Heighton had a certain aura that suggested uncommon reserves of intelligence and insight, a capacity to celebrate his own participation in life hugely rather than just being a small-time celebrity for others, and that's where the resemblance to the young Ondaatje was most pronounced.

When placed alongside one another, their first books of poems persuaded me that Heighton's larger talent was for prose as surely as Ondaatje's was for poetry. And what a large talent for prose Heighton has! There are individual stories in *Flight Paths of the Emperor* that are splendidly intense in their evocation of passions of several sorts (including a passion for particular places on earth) and of the constancy of regret. Both of Heighton's story collections have been republished by Granta in England and he's been translated into French, German and Spanish. That's understandable as soon as you start reading either collection. What isn't quite so comprehensible is that neither book of stories is widely used in Canadian universities so far as I can determine. Heighton's stories are interesting to teach (one or two from *On Earth As It Is* would even be easily subsumed to the kind of thematic criticism Atwoodites pursue) and likely to meet moments of recognition and immediate response from the young in our classrooms who now consider Japan, India and Tibet – common way stations on the road to self-discovery – as normal as the woodlands of the Canadian Shield were to their parents' generation. I keep meeting young writers who want to write about the kinds of things Heighton writes about so well and they have spent whole semesters in creative writing classes dissecting each other's woeful efforts without once being introduced to Heighton's work: that seems to me shameful and scandalous.

In spring 2000, Knopf Canada published Steven Heighton's first novel, *The Shadow Boxer*. It's a book in 'the portrait of the artist' tradition. Sevigne Torrins, an aspiring poet and novelist from northern Ontario, goes to Toronto to 'make it' and discovers the price he must pay to be a creative writer. I was eager to read and review it for the *Globe and Mail*. This is part of what I had to say:

It's Sault Ste Marie, Toronto, and Cairo in the last three decades of the twentieth century as any of us might have experienced them – but this point needs emphasizing because Heighton writes of Sevigne as a son and a lover, a youth confronting the darkness in his own heart in ways that will instantly and alluringly remind some readers not only of Joyce and his descendants but of other novelists from early in the century – D.H. Lawrence and Joseph Conrad and even Thomas Hardy – while leaving others slack-jawed at his lack of literary fashion sense. The old gods have blessed Heighton in ways no post-modern critic ever will: I can't think of another writer in this country – not even Michael Ondaatje – who can be more shockingly *real* while being so mannered. Or so musical. *The Shadow Boxer* is symphonic, Mahler-like in its shifting intensities. What a large talent for cadenced prose Heighton has! Sequences in *The Shadow Boxer* are spine-tingling in their evocation of passions of several sorts (including the desire for particular places on earth) and eye-watering with the constancy of regret.

Heighton continues to confound the prejudices of readers and critics. *The Shadow Boxer* is wonderful and brilliant (we can never have too many novels that are) and, since I wish him well in small things and large, I hope it sells a tonne and wins Steven Heighton a large and loyal following – not for the money it will bring (although I suspect he can use it) but because his large talents are altogether too likely to become crankish with lack of success. In 1997, Heighton published a collection of essays, *The Admen Move on Lhasa: Writing and Culture in a Virtual World* that disappointed expectations when read for pleasure and seemed even thinner when I reread it as a member of the GG non-fiction jury. At its best, it's what Alberto Manguel wrote of it – 'bright, quick, curious, quirky – somewhere between memoirs, musings and late-night café conversations.' But time and again, Heighton puts wrong-footed measures forward. Mark Kingwell, one of the best and brightest of the book reviewers who have now replaced the 'hacks' of Marjorie Harris's time at some of our newspapers, took a hard look at Heighton's essays in the April 26, 1997, *Globe and Mail.* Here's some of what he wrote:

> The title essay sets out the broad distinction to which Heighton will return in various guises, between what he calls 'art', represented somewhat dubiously by the Tibetan city of Lhasa, and 'schlock', a never-defined word that stands in for everything Heighton dislikes: advertising, corporate culture, tourism and consumption. That undefended dichotomy is then paired with galloping, sometimes silly generalizations about human history, on the order of the following: 'The mental separatism which

Plato helped father came back into its own with the Renaissance, picked up steam in the Industrial Revolution, and in our century has set in motion an exponential arc of further abstraction which threatens all life – if not to destroy it altogether, then surely to leach all the poetry and joy from its veins.' ... Throughout these articles, Heighton displays a touching, almost naive, faith in the power of art to ward off the ugliness of contemporary culture, especially the growing 'virtuality' of life and experience. There is also a good deal of complaint, some of it forgivable, concerning the falling stock of artists, especially writers, in a society now given to the quick fix and the Hollywood special effect. In the end, he argues that writers should be 'apostles for the heart,' priests for a secular age.... But missing here is the slow, detail-driven construction of an argument, the careful accumulation of points and evidence that makes for the best kind of thoughtful essay ... Heighton's efforts are not so much essays as outlines for possible ones yet to come. In almost every case, he breaks off just when he has succeeded in snagging the reader's interest, or anyway being irritating enough to provoke attention. And if the prose is sometimes elegantly turned, that only enhances the disappointment that it is deployed to so little purpose.

Perhaps the sketchiness in execution of these themes is a by-product of preaching to the converted from the pulpit-pages of *Brick*, *Malahat Review* or *Quarry* magazine: Heighton has allowed himself the luxury of presuming an audience of similar mind. That's not just unfortunate, it's deadly.

Deadly for readers, *deadening* for writers.

Is it possible to construct a slow, detail-driven argument full of accumulated evidence to support the contention that writers ought to be 'apostles for the heart', priests for a secular age? There are those who say that James Joyce did just that with his creation of Stephen Dedalus in *Portrait of the Artist as a Young Man* and then deconstructed it in *Ulysses*. Denis Sampson reports in *Brian Moore: The Chameleon Novelist* that Moore discovered Joyce when he was eighteen in 1939. Moore wrote, years later:

From those first readings, *Ulysses* changed, if not my life, then my ideas about becoming a writer. It both inspired and intimidated me. It led to a reading of *A Portrait of the Artist* which, for me as for others of my generation became 'our' book, the quintessential Irish *Bildungsroman*, set down brilliantly and unimprovably.

When Moore came to write his first real novel (the thrillers excluded), he did not redo a story of Irish adolescence but Sampson rightly notes that the 'example of Joyce's commitment, however, and the techniques he had developed in *Ulysses* for representing contemporary consciousness in an urban setting became lasting elements of Moore's vocation. That commitment reinforced Moore's own sense of independence from his milieu, and Stephen Dedalus's ringing declaration of his duty to his own self and to his vocation to embrace "silence, exile, and cunning" as a means to becoming an artist undoubtedly fueled Moore's own determination to leave Belfast.'

My article 'You Don't Have to Read Atwood and Her Cadre to Read Canadian' was never published. Virginia Woolf wrote that writers write on a stack of books. The stack of writings upon which I then wrote (topped by Moore's *The Mangan Inheritance*) was not made up of writers who were in fashion. I was crude, too rude in my response to Atwood's work as a critic and to the critics who depended upon it for sinecures of their own: that led me to be overly enthusiastic and uncritical towards some of what I thought ought to replace it. Not getting my article published was a small but real loss in the sense that I regret I wasn't able to do anything to speed up public acceptance of new writing in the eighties – writing that represented contemporary consciousness in an urban setting, that embraced 'silence, exile, and cunning' as a means to becoming an artist and actively supported 'a company of the good'. For reasons that go beyond any desire I might have to appear prescient, I do wish I could say that I'd played some small role in 'discovering' the early work of Brian Fawcett, Keath Fraser, M.T. Kelly, Joy Kogawa, George Szanto. Their early fictions have aged particularly well.

Dull and Very Stiff

'I say why did it take a wee lad to see that the emperor wore no clothes?'
'Well, old son, I'd say nobody else was low down and dirty enough to
keep an eye on the balls.'
— *Jovial John's Smutty Jokebook* (1938)

*'Robertson Davies was the greatest comic novelist in the English language
since Charles Dickens.'*

What? Had I heard right? Well yes, cbc radio quoted John Irving
again on its next arts report when it announced the death of Robertson
Davies in December 1995. This wasn't isolated praise. *Quill & Quire*
mourned the passing of 'Canada's foremost man of letters' and *Books in
Canada* 'the greatest Canadian writer of his generation'. Watching the
Davies memorial service on *Newsworld*, I had to remind myself that
grieving fans will say anything and usually do. A great comic novelist? A
great Canadian writer? I couldn't remember encountering him as either.
Then again, I'd stopped reading Davies in the mid-eighties. In 1986,
Norman Snider's 'Robertson Davies: The View from High Table' in *The
Bumper Book* put a finger right on what seemed to be Davies' deepest
flaw, his self-righteous sentimentality:

> Davies is the newest master of what has been called the novel of
> resignation ... Davies knows the Upper Canadian village at its
> narrow worst. He is not concerned with liberation from its limits
> but with the acceptance by his characters of the authentic sense of
> the nature it has imposed on them ... this sentiment extends to
> Davies' futility of Canada leaving behind its colonial mentality
> and moving into its own as a nation ... Davies' most dominant
> emotion is pietistic.

Davies had nothing to say to Canadian nationalists with names like
mine, and Quebec, where I've chosen to live, doesn't exactly need to
import pious regard for village idiocies from Upper Canada. So I

45

hadn't read his last three novels or thought about the others until the previous year when I read Judith Skelton Grant's very thick biography, *Robertson Davies: Man of Myth*. It stirred an old memory: when I was fifteen, irritation with Davies' Salterton novels kick-started me into a permanent and useful scepticism towards *Saturday Night* – approved CanLit. I owed Davies *something*, and the only thing any writer deserves is to be read attentively. During the first months of 1996, I read all eleven novels.

It was a rocky ride. The novels are unevenly paced, implausibly plotted, shamelessly self-aggrandizing. Davies as novelist didn't grow from strength to strength and then fall into decline. His most accomplished fiction, *Fifth Business* (1970), was followed immediately by *The Manticore* (1972) which was nearly as inept as *A Mixture of Frailties* (1958). He reached bottom with *Murther and Walking Spirits* (1991) and then rose to *The Cunning Man* (1994) his last but second-best novel. Overtly didactic and deliberately offensive to democratic, socialist and egalitarian sensibilities, these novels are humorous in the grumpy way of one for whom night life is no kind of life and the body is a burden in need of feeding and purging rather than a blessing. His books are pervaded by condescending, complacent, nostalgic, mostly male intellectuals who aren't particularly intelligent but are single, solvent, cerebral and get very stiff contemplating the status quo of an Anglo Canada in which there is no room for most of us. Quirky more than comic, they are diverting: *The Rebel Angels* ranks as one of the most tedious novels of the second half of the century, but the sub-plot about how old violins get restored kept me turning pages long after I'd ceased being even remotely interested in any of the characters. That's harmless enough amusement and I didn't begrudge myself its distraction. Nor do I begrudge anyone else the right to gorge themselves on a steady dose of Davies. I just don't think these novels offer any reason to be taken *seriously* as comic literature. As John Metcalf says:

> Davies is essentially a very *middlebrow* entertainer like, say, J.B. Priestley. His appeal is to people who know nothing of his subject matter but are titillated by the easily-acquired esotericism. Just as readers of Dennis Wheatley were titillated by odd bits of witchcraft lore and the odd Latin tag. They derive from all this

nonsense the feeling that they're being allowed in on the inside.

After the first three novels, I copped out on reading the remainder in chronological order. The Salterton trilogy of *Tempest-Tost* (1951), *Leaven of Malice* (1954), and *A Mixture of Frailties* (1958) is even more sententious, xenophobic and misogynous than I remembered. After them, I cut to *Murther and Walking Spirits* (1991) and *A Cunning Man* (1994) before going back to the Cornish trilogy of *The Rebel Angels* (1981), *What's Bred in the Bone* (1985) and *The Lyre of Orpheus* (1988), ending with the celebrated Deptford trilogy of *Fifth Business* (1970), *The Manticore* (1972), and *World of Wonders* (1975). This mixing-up was small relief, something like adding extra cream when you're shaving your throat with a dull blade: the later novels are frothier and slicker but still very scratchy underneath. I persevered out of perplexity: How could anyone equate Davies with Dickens?

Except for beard and theatrical mannerisms, delight in cosiness and a propensity to sentimentality, Dickens and Davies can't be seen in continuity in any meaningful way unless you twist your head into a choke hold and knock yourself out. As a literary critic, John Irving makes a fine wrestler. Davies gets easy laughs from some set pieces but his talent for sketching the horrors of provincial life through a monocle doesn't make him comic at the level of James Joyce, Flann O'Brien, P.G. Wodehouse, Evelyn Waugh, Angus Wilson, Joseph Heller, Kingsley Amis, Mordecai Richler – to name only a few *comic* novelists who rank much higher.

When you read Dickens, you get a symphonic sense of spoken English, the interplay of whole sections of the class system, a counterpoint of trios and quartets, soaring soloists: there are horns, woodwinds, strings, brasses and percussion, old instruments and new in two distinct genders but with gradations of sexual difference. Dickens and Mahler and Picasso can all be mentioned in the same breath as masters of tonality. Dickens and Davies?

After bowing and scraping at a fiddle of Trollope in the Salterton books, Davies' characters all sound like they've been taught to speak by Dunstan Ramsay, the narrator of *Fifth Business* and the only fully realized character Davies produced. David Staunton and Paul Dempster, the centres of the other Deptford novels, are indistinguishable from one another and from Ramsay. When Davies uses alternating narrators in *The Rebel Angels*, there's no discernible difference between Maria Magdelena Theotoky, a twenty-five-year-old graduate student of gypsy background and European mother tongues, and Simon Darcourt, a middle-aged Anglican priest, who is Ramsay once again. Here's Maria Magdelena describing her relations with her parents and with men:

> I was half Gypsy, and since my Father died the half sometimes seemed in my Mother's estimation to amount to three-quarters, or even seven-eighths. I knew she loved me deeply, but like any deep love there were times when I was a burden, and its demands cruel. To live with my Mother meant living according to her beliefs, which were in almost every way at odds with what I had learned elsewhere. It had been different when my Father was alive, because he could control her, not by shouting or domination – that was her way – but by the extraordinary force of his noble character.
>
> He was a very great man, and since his death when I was sixteen I had been looking for him, or something like him, among all the men I met. I believe that psychiatrists explain such a search as mine to troubled girls as though it were a deep secret the girls could never have uncovered for themselves, but I had always known it; I wanted my Father, I wanted to find a man who was his equal in bravery and wisdom and warmth of love, and once or twice, briefly, I thought I had found him in Clement Hollier. Wisdom I knew he possessed; if it were called for I was sure he would have bravery; warmth of love was what I wanted to arouse in him, but I knew it would never do to thrust myself at him. I must serve; I must let my love be seen in humility and sacrifice; I must let him discover me.

The result is hilarious in ways the author didn't intend. Ultimately, Ramsay becomes the voice of Heaven itself as the Recording Angel in *What's Bred in the Bone*. Moulded by Upper Canada College, they've all run aground in the mid-Atlantic on the upper decks of the last of the pre-war ocean liners.

The gulf between Davies and Dickens goes deeper than the fact that

Dickens has an ear for speech and employs English with a complexity, richness, and density that comes close to Shakespeare, while Davies can't get beyond Ramsay's inflated Edwardian rhetoric except with a parlour impersonation of Rabelais as stiff as a soiled lace antimacassar. Dickens confided to his friend George Lewes that he literally *heard* every word uttered by his characters with such force that he had to record them, scribe-like, without regard for the impact they made on his own literary vision or sense of language. Because of this receptiveness, Dickens doesn't possess a master imagination, a *system* that holds his experiences together for conscience to examine. As Lord Acton said, Dickens knows nothing of sin when it isn't a crime. Davies is all system, a conscientious Jungian who examines sin with the scruples of an Oxford Movement Anglican. Dickens knows evil and deals with the exploitation of one person by another and the systematic despoliation of human decency by financial and legal systems that legitimize greed. Davies is all for decency but seems to think that all's right with the world so long as banks pay steady rates of interest and the devil gets whoever purloins the family silver. In Dickens, characters plunge straight into life, virtuously or viciously: the virtuous don't turn evil but the villains do stand naked in terrible aloneness and die with full knowledge of their fears and weaknesses. This is the source of Dickens's optimism and comedy: we laugh in the face of the most grotesque circumstances because it's the real world and we're all in it together. Dickens's comedy is inclusive, not dismissive. This is the very thing that makes Dickens so effective a critic of snobbery: in *Great Expectations*, Dickens lays bare the manner in which a dream of a genteel life is grounded in the desire to possess, maintain and cherish a lover who is so beautiful, brilliant, delicate, and refined as to be eternally fresh and unsullied by any kind of work. Then he shows just how easily such a dream turns the dreamer into his own favourite object of desire. Davies glories in just such self-regard.

John Irving isn't the only one to insist on Davies' dubious connection to Dickens. Judith Skelton Grant dottily compares Davies' childhood in Renfrew, Ontario, as the much petted youngest son of a man of growing wealth and political influence, to Dickens's experiences in a blacking factory when his own father was in debtor's prison. Davies seems to have seldom done a lick of physical labour, and it shows: he can't draw a detailed portrait of anybody who isn't of the managerial class, and workers are treated with remorseless disdain. Unlike Dickens, he has no idea how hard work grinds the body and scours spirits it doesn't murder. Labour and poverty didn't interest Davies. They're drab, and Robertson Davies was the dandy son of a flamboyant man.

Senator Rupert Davies (1879–1967) emigrated from Wales as a poor and unskilled youth, became a printer's apprentice and ended up owning the Kingston *Whig-Standard*, the Peterborough *Examiner* and various radio and television stations. He lived splendidly as a would-be aristocrat in a manor house in Wales every summer and spent his winters in Ottawa fomenting political intrigues. He meddled incorrigibly in the lives of his three sons while endowing them and their offspring with pots of money. The meddling included getting Robertson admitted to Queen's University as a non-degree student on a reduced course load after he'd failed to fully matriculate from Upper Canada College. Senator Davies then managed to get his youngest boy into Balliol College, Oxford, without benefit of proper qualifications in Latin or much else.

When Vincent Massey handpicked Robertson Davies to be the first Master of Massey College (which carried with it an appointment to a professorship in the University of Toronto and teaching duties in the faculty of graduate studies) despite his conspicuous lack of any academic credential other than a B.Litt. he'd acquired when the pursuit of an Oxford B.A. proved too strenuous, many members of the university were aghast. However, Senator Rupert Davies was pleased, 'Oh, you must do that! You mustn't let that go by! It will raise you right above trade!'

Becoming a highly placed academic and a celebrated novelist came second to Davies' lifelong affair with the theatre. His obsession with the stage undermines his novels just as it allegedly subverted attempts to educate him. After his very minor job at the Old Vic was cancelled by the war and Davies returned to Canada in 1940, he became a workaholic who edited the Peterborough *Examiner*, wrote twice-weekly columns as Samuel Marchbanks and another syndicated column under his own name, and reviewed books at *Saturday Night* while acting and directing in amateur theatre at every opportunity. Set on becoming a celebrated London playwright, he poured what he considered his best energy and greatest skills into writing plays. The results are theatre pieces that were decidedly out of touch with the sense, sensibilities or sense of nonsense of people who'd survived the Blitz. Davies started writing novels only when it became clear that nobody of any stature wanted to produce any of his plays. *Tempest-Tost* gives a fair idea of Davies the playwright, since it's really a novelization of a three-act country house comedy. All it lacks is a butler named Jeeves and Wodehouse's larger talent and better nature.

Davies was born with one skin too few or maybe it was just flailed off by the Senator. The lack of a cape of theatrical acclaim or an overcoat of academic respectability made Davies easily abraded, itching to put the world in its place. Whatever else Davies might have intended his first three novels to do, he gets his own back on people who wronged him during his adolescence in Kingston, teachers and women in particular. And he's very particular: if the dead could sue for libel, his books would be much thinner than they are. The result is savage comedy that's too personal and childish to be satire. It's a crude burlesque of the world of grown-up women performed with an adolescent boy's sneer. When they aren't villainous mothers or treacherous girlfriends, the females in Davies' novels are just some variant on a good old boy in drag. Given that most of his men are bachelors, there's no real sexual tension and no complex passion in any of the novels. Whenever he pisses on his female characters, Davies mostly wets his own trousers. Abjectly.

At the age of forty-seven, when Davies put editing the *Examiner* and writing novels aside to become the first Master of Massey College, it wasn't all hijinks at high table and celebrating *faux antique* college traditions. During his term as Canada's first native-born Governor General, Vincent Massey had decided an Oxford enclosure at the University of Toronto was the most satisfactory way of celebrating his own slant on life and commemorating the family name emblazoned on tens of thousands of farm implements. He intended Massey College to civilize select male graduate students by providing them with residential accommodation, companionship with senior scholars at meals, exposure to the arts and outside contacts with men of affairs. Massey was an imperious Anglophile with a penchant for formal dress, elaborate ceremonies and off-colour jokes. He wanted a Master in his own image and Davies was the closest thing to hand. Massey expected Davies to be his mouthpiece and a lackey of the Massey Trust. Judith Skelton Grant makes light of the way Davies played both roles admirably during his first decade at Massey. She excuses his lack of respect for the rights of students, his arrogant and secretive handling of college business, his vociferous male chauvinism, and his virulent dispute with Professor W.A.C.H. Dobson as just part of the silliness of the sixties. Times changed, attitudes changed, Massey died, Senator Davies died, and Robertson Davies changed.

He did. His years at Massey wound his irritability up several notches and set it off in new directions in the novels while he developed the persona for which he became so well known. The Deptford and Cornish trilogies are the counter-attack and revenge of a writer dedicated to holding up his academic credentials while defecating on the graves of his enemies: the thoroughly vicious attack on Professor Dobson (his nemesis at Massey College, who's thinly veiled as Nasty McVarish in *The Rebel Angels*) is a particularly grotesque and excessive example of literary gay-bashing. When Davies isn't savaging his enemies in these six novels, he's defending his shady nook in the groves of academe. Talk-laden, they read like Iris Murdoch at her most leaden, taking tea with John Henry Cardinal Newman, J.B. Priestley and assorted West End playwrights, with everybody talking of T.S. Eliot's experiments in drama and C.G. Jung's theories of psychological growth in the house Thomas Mann built on the foundation of E.T.A. Hoffman's tales. What's truly amazing is how well Davies manages to pull it off in *Fifth Business*, his most focused book and only substantial claim to serious attention as a novelist.

While Davies was writing *Fifth Business*, he was widely regarded as a *poseur* in university circles. But Iris Murdoch was quite well regarded in those same places because of her ability to transpose the high art of T.S. Eliot's plays into the minor key of the British popular novel without seeming to betray her calling as professor of philosophy at Oxford. Murdoch's attempts to express ultimate themes of man's search for truth and the conflict between good and evil through ritualistic actions performed by stock figures of the London stage (who turn themselves inside out to reveal unexpected depths of poetic intensity and beauty) put a neat spin on sitting-room melodrama. In *A Severed Head* (1961), which became the kind of hit on the London stage that Davies most envied, Murdoch creates a businessman narrator with an avocation for history who gives credibility to Murdoch's own academic pursuits. Dunstan Ramsay narrates *Fifth Business* as a historian with a head for business who applies hagiography to the study of popular saints in a manner very like the one Davies used in his studies of nineteenth century romance and melodrama at University of Toronto. *A Severed Head* provided so nice an example of academically acceptable novel-making that Davies uses its central image in the magic act crucial to the plot of *Fifth Business* and models Liesl Vitzlipützli on Murdoch's Honor Klein right down to physical appearance, wrestling skills, and psychological effect on the narrator. This insight into Murdoch's influence isn't my own: it comes from Michael Peterman's *Robertson Davies* (1986). Peterman is an astute critic who captures the flaws of the first seven novels but still reveres Davies. In 'The Acts of Robertson Davies' (*Books in Canada*, February 1996), he writes:

> His life is truly an exhilarating story of the way a man and an artist can, out of his inner needs, ambition, and capacity for work, make himself over to meet the world, and do so at different stages of life, each time with increasing cogency and purpose.... With an artist's ego and a sustaining fascination in life and its mysteries, he not only provided a set of warnings about the country's need for a richer cultural life but he showed how a committed vision could minister to those needs.

Indeed? In *Fifth Business*, Dunstan Ramsay (whose initials are a reversal of Robertson Davies) is motivated to write his memoirs because Ramsay wants readers to know that he has lived a good life by cultivating egoism, confounding the mob, and committing himself to vitalizing a few others as a master in a boys' school. Follow destiny and you'll find wonderful help along the way and ultimately win the admiration of the only people who truly matter, Ramsay says. Ramsay becomes the perfect vehicle for everything Davies wants to say about himself and his role as Master of Massey College: the true artist is a magus in an academic gown who relieves pressures within the managerial class by turning troubled young men into self-reliant old boys by mind-fucking them into self-knowledge.

Responding to tributes paid him in 1989 at Harbourfront's International Author's Festival, Davies told his audience that Samuel Johnson and James Boswell came to him in a dream and persuaded him *not* to write his autobiography, because he had done nothing but write all his life, his happy marriage could not be explored without violating conjugal privacies, he had no military exploits to relate, and he'd not acquired any great fortune. It was characteristic stagecraft, less genuine than disingenuous, immodestly modest. Davies inflates himself by confessing to intimacy with the shades of Johnson and Boswell and then lets *them* suggest his writing places him in their company. It doesn't: Boswell wrote of Johnson and Johnson wrote of many things, but Davies never got beyond himself and bits of Ontario as a country doctor might perceive it.

Dr Johnson would have dismissed Davies as too inconsequential to merit any attention, had he known him, but Boswell would have been fascinated. Davies was a rich man's son tied tightly to paternal purse strings. Few things were more interesting to Boswell than autocratic fathers and the presence of their money in the lives of their sons. Boswell would also have been consumed with interest in the larger fact that Davies lived out a long life with a greater degree of financial security, domestic stability, loyal friendship, public acclaim, and freedom to travel than any writer of Dr Johnson's era and most of our own, without ever giving up a dreadful need to exact revenge on those less fortunate. Boswell would have been fascinated, but he would not have been filled with admiration: he saved that for Dr Johnson and David Hume.

In 1959, when I first worked my way through the Salterton novels, I discovered guilty pleasure in the act of reading Davies. I didn't find Davies naughty, *risqué,* nudge-nudge: I'd already read *Peyton Place* and Davies never put tit in his titillations. No, it was embarrassing but stimulating to find myself in the presence of an older man who was dumber than I was when it came to the real world. I knew nothing of Davies, and little beyond Saskatchewan, but what I knew told me that what he'd constructed in the Salterton novels was a house of marked cards, a cheat of self-pity, and a swindle of supercilious twaddle that raised itself up by denigrating everything else. And it toppled as soon as I compared it to the latest book from the other Canadian writer I'd discovered that same year. *The Apprenticeship of Duddy Kravitz* was Mordecai Richler's fourth novel and in trying to figure out how and why Richler was a better writer, I took the advice of a librarian at the Regina Public Library and found my way to Kingsley Amis and Evelyn Waugh: both led me to see that despite all their substantial differences from Dickens, they're in continuity with him, and Davies is not.

I hate the journalistic fashion of identifying our common culture as belonging to one generation or another. The inability of Davies to speak to us in any important way throughout the last third of the twentieth century has little to do with the fact that he was seventeen when Richler was born and thirty-two when the first baby boomers came into the world, and much to do with the fact that Davies, like his great hero Jung, was insensitive to the lives of women and minorities living right in front of him and very incautious in describing archetypes. Davies gives comfort to complacency: Richler does not. And that's why it's Richler, not Davies, who has been Canada's 'foremost *man* of letters' through the past forty years. Richler has neglected nothing essential of his time in this place and uses his own thin skin to goad our consciences – no other Canadian has written with greater cogency over a greater range. And he's damned funny. Whenever I read Richler, I just say, 'Here we are, this is *us*.' That simply doesn't happen with Davies. As a novelist, Davies seems to write of many things, but his fictions emerge mainly out of a tension between being himself and being Senator Davies' son, between being an actor in his own play and being a puppet in his father's hands. The result is a series of tales in which Davies tries too earnestly to become what he once described his father as being, 'the Lord God Almighty, all the bards of Wales, the Devil, Mr Micawber, Charlie Chaplin ...' It's his battle to gain ascendency over his father's world that made Davies appear so much older than he actually was. After *Fifth Business*, Davies himself seemed to join Dunstan Ramsay's generation (which is nearly the Senator's) and assume chunks of that personality in public appearances. But it irritated Davies to be thought old-maidish and old-fashioned, and he was forever pouring Ramsay into new bottles by shaping his books according to contemporary theatrical devices and adding new and more esoteric ornamentation. It still surprises me that Anthony Burgess devoured these novels without choking. Then again, anything new and full enough of food and drink to let Burgess fantasize about lurid bodily excretions distracted him beyond all reason. One of the more delicious ironies literary life offers is that fans of Davies turn to Burgess for confirmation of Davies' stature: Burgess is the very paradigm of the abundantly talented and sexually voracious but morally flawed intellectual unable to form consistently true judgements that Davies savaged, from Revelstoke in *A Mixture of Frailties* to Parlabane in *The Rebel Angels*.

John Irving can place Robertson Davies right alongside Charles Dickens on his bookshelf as much as he likes but Davies just isn't comparable to any nineteenth-century English novelist: their main characters are focal points but aren't central to the action in the way the first-person narrators are in Davies' non-Salterton novels. Dickens, Eliot, Thackeray, and Trollope depict male and female characters who acquire self-knowledge by learning to discriminate between the false and the genuine, the evil and the good in the people and public institutions with which they're in contact. Davies' narrators grind out propaganda on behalf of his own self-serving evaluation of the social utility of art and the artist for the managerial elite.

As a novelist, Davies was an indifferent craftsman. He wrote unevenly. His tales were guided by a view of twentieth-century man that it's only wishful thinking to call 'antiquated': it remains all too current among those who think there is some wisdom to be found in neo-conservatism. Like Joseph Campbell, that other celebrated popularizer of C.G. Jung, Robertson Davies helps legitimize the rise of ideology at the expense of serious thinking about the fix we're in. His celebrated 'carnival' is a Punch-and-Judy show in which it's the audience that gets clobbered.

I never met Davies, nor did I enter Massey College during his tenure as Master, and don't have any intimate connection to anyone who did. I'm prepared to believe the nice things Judith Skelton Grant says about Davies as a man, even if her biography, *Robertson Davies: Man of Myth*, offers readers a small-town girl's hagiographic view of Davies as Presence, a sort of Blessed Sacrament for the Perpetually Not-Quite-Sophisticated, dispensing small acts of mannered graciousness and large doses of garrulity. I'm even prepared to concede Michael Peterman's claim that the novels don't do full justice to either the character or the talent of Robertson Davies. But that's just the point! Literature is an art. Those who are great artists are often imperfect models. It's the attempt to deny

56

the distinctness of art from artifice and morality from moralism that makes the novels of Robertson Davies so *objectionable* and *abject*.

Most of the foregoing appeared in the Autumn 1997 issue of *Paragraph*. Have I had any second thoughts since then? Not at all. But to judge from the November/December 1998 issue of *Books in Canada*, Professor Michael Peterson has. In his review of *The Merry Heart: Selections 1980-1995* and *Happy Alchemy: Writings on the Theatre and Other Lively Arts*, the two posthumous collections of Robertson Davies' material that McClelland & Stewart have published to date, Peterson notes:

> No matter what the subject – the novel, literacy, Canadian public policy, Jung, technology, opera, Christmas, old age or even Mavis Gallant – he was always most concerned with two things: himself and his sense of things as a writer. While this was the predictable recourse of a man who knew that his novels had earned him wide acclaim and a large readership, what one sees here from essay to essay is a repeated pattern that seems more static than alive, and how the process of individuation turns into prickly self-absorption and mannered response ... he takes us nowhere in a leisurely, drifting fashion. Which is fine if one is inclined to see oneself among his privileged elite. However, if one looks for a convincing argument, if one objects to the falsities of emphasis, if one looks for a depth of insight that awakens understanding, or encourages further thinking, one may well be disappointed. One may in fact be inclined to agree with Davies when, with ingenuous rhetorical sweep, he says to his Yale audience, 'How dull he is being, you may think, as I draw to my conclusion.'

Peterson notes at the beginning of his essay what a triumph – organizers had to turn away nearly as many as they seated – Robertson Davies had in New York City when he read from *A Cunning Man*. I note without further comment that Robertson Davies and his works are nowhere to be found in the 647 pages of *Books of the Century: A Hundred Years of Authors, Ideas and Literature from The New York Times*.

At Morton Rosengarten's Vernissage, 1966

In the Wings

In late April 1992, I interviewed Carole Corbeil for the Montreal *Gazette*. She was on a triumphal trip back to her old home town as a literary celebrity. Her first novel, *Voice-over*, was on several Canadian best-seller lists and she was having a lot more fun than serious writers are supposed to have when they have just broken into print. The response to *Voice-over* had been nothing short of phenomenal. On sale barely a month, it was already being called a 'classic' by very credible people. Carole Corbeil was receiving the kind of media coverage that's usually reserved only for well-established, award-winning literary lions.

I met with her over coffee in a Westmount bistro between her appearances on local radio shows. She'd already given five or six interviews that day and was struggling a little to catch her breath and collect her thoughts but she was smiling as she said, 'All this attention! It's like going from famine to feast. You're alone for so long and then whoosh, you're out of the gate.'

She was leading the pack from an odd position. *Voice-over* doesn't have what one generally expects to find in a book that captures the public imagination – a strong plot. What it does have is an emotional trajectory that sweeps readers up into the world of Claudine Beaulieu, an angry Québécoise documentary film-maker, and the WASP literary con man in her life in Toronto in the mid-eighties. 'I found that I had to be really true to those characters and their emotional states. My biggest discovery was that emotional honesty has a narrative drive in itself because this is actually quite a fragmented book. There is something about it like a broken mirror and all the pieces are reflecting one another. It amazes me that people read it through and get into it despite the lack of any real plot.'

I wasn't at all amazed. Claudine's life is compelling both in itself and in relation to her mother's in Montreal during the fifties and sixties. *Voice-over* is a deft portrait of women of two very different generations discovering truths about themselves in the interplay of languages and cultures. The book is full of close observations that make readers nod with instant recognition. Besides, I told her, Claudine seemed to me to be a sister to a lot of the attractive, talented, bilingual women I see on Radio Canada and C B C, except that she's much angrier and less tolerant of fatuous male behaviour. 'A guy at Radio Canada called me up and he was doing a review of the book and he couldn't get over how angry she is. He just found her so angry and intransigent. She doesn't let anybody get away with anything. I don't think I could have created a clearer context for why she is the way she is. It made me feel that maybe in Quebec, women can't really be angry yet. Do you know what I mean?'

I wasn't altogether certain I did. Not then. Eight years later, I think her sense of this was on-target. The night of our meeting, *Voice-over* was given a launch by Bill Dodge over on Duluth Street at Montreal's most interesting bookstore of that period, the late and lamented *Ficciones*. The small space was crowded with about as many people as could squeeze in before serious oxygen deprivation starts to occur. Carole Corbeil read two short passages from her book. She was spectacularly attractive in tight black pants and camisole covered by an elegant frock coat of many colours. Her voice was small, light and compelling as she recounted a courtship scene set in the early fifties between Claudine's parents-to-be in a new Studebaker on Mont Royal. She followed this with a scene from a part of the book people were already referring to familiarly as 'The Dinner Party from Hell'.

My judgement that people really like her writing was amply confirmed. Not just by her old friends from Westmount and Outremont. From where I stood, I could spot a few of the better book reviewers in Montreal and they were unusually attentive. 'Where did she come from?' the literary hustler beside me asked. 'I've never heard of her,' said he who prides himself on knowing everybody who's published anything in even the smallest of literary magazines.

'Newspapers.'

Like most overnight sensations, Carole Corbeil had paid her dues. For the previous several years, she had been a freelance writer and editor in Toronto. Before that, she was a regular columnist covering the visual arts and dance for the *Globe and Mail*. Some time before that, she was at the *Gazette* where she hadn't managed to get a crack at any job beyond taking advertisements for the classifieds. Corbeil has been writing since her adolescence but she'd told me over coffee that she didn't really find her voice as a novelist until after the birth of her daughter in the mid-eighties. 'It really focused me. It brought back to me what I'd started to forget. What I want my readers to remember is how mingled the French and English were in their everyday lives. This is an interesting legacy to explore of the years before Mulroney.'

It certainly was. *Voice-over* does what good novels always do – it gives new and very specific insights into a small story that throws unexpected light upon much larger issues. *Voice-over* asks what's gained and what's lost when a native Montrealer adopts Toronto as her home town. It's a question most Montrealers of my acquaintance have asked themselves too many times as more than a few friends, lovers, children have taken the 401 solution to their personal and professional problems and the political solutions advocated by Québécois nationalists. *Voice-over* is set in the summer of 1984 and Claudine Beaulieu has successfully transplanted her Quebec-bred talent as a documentary film-maker into the heart of anglo-phoniness. Her films of women at the margins of society – prostitutes, prison inmates – have earned her a secure middle-of-the-political-spectrum reputation in the Toronto arts community but her personal life is as fragmented, torn-up and wasted as clips of film on the editing-room floor. Her primary relationship is with a punkish poet, a *poseur* such as only Upper Canada College can produce although Lower Canada College runs a mean second. They live together without sharing any kind of life beyond that which can be fuelled by cocaine or booze or jealousy. Together, they are vile in more ways than they could ever manage on their own.

What makes Claudine worthwhile and affecting and gives her life an interest beyond simple voyeurism is the tenuous connection she maintains with Janine, her sister, a suburban housewife married to a house renovator, and their divorced parents. And what parents these sisters have! In the days before the Quiet Revolution, Odette O'Shea wed Roger Beaulieu and became a perfect wife to a badly flawed husband and a charming mother to Claudine and her sister, Janine. As Beaulieu sank deeper into debt and alcoholism, Odette held the family together by selling her cool blond Grace Kelly looks to Radio Canada television advertisers. And when her looks faded and the marriage finally failed, she remarried into Westmount money and privilege and carried her daughters with her – losing a language, gaining golf. Now, while Odette succumbs to Valium trances at a luxury retirement villa in Jamaica, Roger rages against the English in Montreal as both compete for the adult love of their daughters.

Corbeil intercuts the stories of Claudine and her mother so that their struggles, gains and losses are mirrored in one another and magnified in the smaller presences of Janine and Roger. It is a deft and incisive portrait of women of two very different generations discovering the truth about themselves in the interplay of two cities and two cultures. Like her heroine, the author has made the journey from Montreal to Toronto and French to English. And while she'd told me she didn't feel at home anywhere, she made me as a reader feel very much at home inside both the languages that take one inside Claudine's skin. Montrealers – francophone and anglophone, native-born and adopted – are much more the children of one family than is often realized. A book like *Voice-over* drops its hook into waters far beyond the shallows of most political journalism to make that point in an unforgettable fashion. It's easy enough to say that we who live on this languorous island in the middle of the St. Lawrence in the heartland of a forest, with eyes open to the Gulf and the old world beyond, are *baguette et vin*, mysteriously consecrated and cursed sisters and brothers, but Carole Corbeil illuminates this truth with emotional fireworks of a very high order.

The relationship between Claudine on cocaine and her poet on booze neatly skewers all such relationships. After reading *Voice-over*, no one should be able to look at a guy with a bunch of poems stuffed inside his black leather jacket in quite the same romantic way as before. The relationship between Claudine and her sister is equally well done – as well done, in fact, as sisters have been done in a novel in this country since Barbara Gowdy's splendid *Falling Angels* in 1989. Indeed, Corbeil's ability to capture a sense of the emotional tone of Toronto in the eighties in clean, clear, compressed prose is matched only, I think, by Gowdy and M.T. Kelly. It's certainly not writing for those who want to sentimentalize things. It's writing for those who can lament and celebrate more than the opening and closing times of bars and the balances in our bank accounts. *Voice-over* does what good novels always do: it smartens us up while moving us deeply. And it does it with more French dialogue than I had thought a Toronto publisher was willing to risk even in the early nineties.

At the end of our interview, I asked Carole Corbeil what she was working on. She told me that it was a novel about a group of actors putting on one of Shakespeare's plays. '*Tempest-Tost* for our times? Not that I think anybody is ever going to mistake you for Robertson Davies,' I joked. She stopped smiling.

I'm told by a mutual friend that Carole Corbeil found it very hard to smile in 1998, the year following publication of her intellectually playful and emotionally challenging second novel, *In the Wings*. *Voice-over* had not only stayed on the best-seller lists for some weeks but it also was shortlisted for both the W.H. Smith First Novel Award and the Trillium Book Award, and won the City of Toronto Book award. *In the Wings*, a more accomplished and complex work, chased Mordecai Richler's *Barney's Version* down to the Caribbean for the regional final of the Commonwealth Prize but failed to make an impact on the juries for either the Governor General's Literary Award or the Giller Prize or on the public via best-seller status. This despite sizeable advertisements. The design department at Stoddart did the book no favour by featuring a cherub and human skull on a sepia dust jacket and, worse, their promotion department does have something to answer for by trivializing *In the Wings* in terms that tiredly convey something less than the heart of a very vital book that has absolutely nothing in common with a soap opera:

Allan O'Reilly is a young actor on the cusp of a brilliant career when he meets Alice Riverton on the set of a forgettable movie. Alice, almost 40, almost successful, had escaped to Los Angeles after a disastrous affair with a married man, but her mother's sudden death brings her back to Toronto. Scheduled to play Gertrude in an upcoming production of *Hamlet*, Alice falls in love with Allan and sweeps him into her world. Their intense relationship, already strained by the weight of their separate griefs – Allan has not come to terms with the death of his father – shifts calamitously when Allan is cast as Hamlet. Carole Corbeil's new novel is a passionate and lyrical exploration of how art informs life – how a script as ancient as *Hamlet* can haunt those who set about to revive and relive it. In this rich exploration of life, love, and the theatre world, language that was written 400 years ago pushes like a glacier through one actor's psyche and sets his own past in motion. A play is never just a play; it is the story of what happens to the actors while making the play come alive.

Compare that and all of its predictable modifiers with this sample of Corbeil's own prose. Here is Allan, depressed, riding the King streetcar from the corner of Parliament:

... as the doors fold behind him, sees himself as if he were watching the streetcar from outside, a dark figure lunging about in a bright tube.

Sitting down, he looks at the fine veins of his wrists.

White light on his wrists. Smell of wet wool. Ads with beautiful women licking their lips. Outside, old territory clattering by. Used to walk here with his father when Nate and he were boys. His father had this drill when they were walking. He'd say, where are we, boys? Look around you. Where are we? On this old street that was once close to the lake they'd say, York, sir. Muddy York.

Peel it back, boys, King Street is an old Indian trail.

The Mississauga tribe sold a hundred thousand hectares of this land for ten shillings to the government of Upper Canada.

And what's a shilling, Dad, one of them would ask.

Pocket change. Think about it, boys, this land has gone from hunting to agriculture to real estate in less than two hundred years. It's not just history that's under there, but a whole way of life. They paved a whole way of life.

Such regret and rage poured out of their father's voice that they wanted to make the world over for him.

Let's bomb the town, Dad, Nate would say, let's pour gasoline all over the place and torch it. And Allan would see the conflagration in his mind, the town reduced to charcoal and the three of them canoeing on the Don River, roasting small birds over an open fire for lunch.

His wrists ache. He thinks of what it would be like to cut them. Cut sideways, not across.

This is just one of the modes Corbeil uses to establish – without purple patches, excess padding or pretentiousness – the many layers in the lives of her characters and the city they live in and that comes to life through them.

In the Wings revolves around a down-to-the-last-of-its-funding Toronto theatre company's desperate attempt to save itself from ruin by staging William Shakespeare's *Hamlet*. Corbeil interweaves the stories of three characters who are haunted by loving relationships they have lost. Allan O'Reilly, who is cast as Hamlet, comes by his depression genetically: his father, recently deceased, was a manic depressive and his father's self-torment is never further away than the blood throbbing in his own wrists. Alice Riverton, who is to play Queen Gertrude, has returned to Toronto from Los Angeles for the funeral of her mother. Robert Pullwarden, the drama critic for Toronto's largest newspaper, is separated from his wife who immediately moved to Vancouver to maximize the distance between not just the two of them but also between Pullwarden and his beloved infant son. Pullwarden is also mad with lust for Louise Martin, a very young actress. Alice is failing to stay free of men who do her no good. Allan is feeding his manic side and staving off depression as best he can by using women and being used by them. The struggles of these central characters and the other minor players with one another and with their roles within the play that becomes more and more part of their lives is framed in prologue and epilogue by a character who is more bereft than any of them, the unnamed child of Allan and Alice who lets us know from the outset that the tales we are to be told all end in more tears than laughter. It's the voice of a haunted child summoning ghosts back to the stage to play once more the parts that failed to bring Hamlet's Denmark back to brilliant life on the stage of the Phoenix Theatre but succeeded too well in bringing death, destruction and only a fragile breath of new life to a small corner of Toronto. It's the presence of the narrator at beginning and end that brings to *In the Wings* an expansion of the device of a play within a play that rivals the complexities of the trial within a trial in Mordecai Richler's *St. Urbain's Horseman*. And like Richler at his best, Corbeil manages to bring into the main tale all sorts of reflections and commentaries on eroticism, domesticity, loneliness, obsessiveness, aging, religion, writing, reviewing and Canadianism without making a misstep and knocking the whole out of shape.

Corbeil, who is married to the stage actor Layne Coleman (who has played Hamlet), knows the theatre world and Toronto's actors at least as well as Richler knows the world of scriptwriters and Canadian expatriates in London. Everything in her book is apposite and feels authentic. Her dialogue is very spare but effective. Here's Allan in conversation with his girlfriend, Kristen:

'I got some smoked salmon,' he said.
'I wish,' she said.
'What?'
'I wish you wouldn't. It costs a fortune and you don't even like it. You like the idea of it, but you don't eat it.'
'I get it for you. It's gold.'
'Oh, Allan.'
'What? And there's this beautiful blueberry jam?'
'What was the part? Do you think you got it?'
Allan froze. He hated it when she took his career on. Kristen was as aggressive with his career as she was passive about hers.
'The usual,' he said. 'Good-looking guy. Rebellious. Needs to learn how to love.'
'Come on.'
'I'm serious. It actually says that in the specs.'
'Who's to love?'
'They've already cast her, honey. Sorry.'

She put the bacon on a plate and brought it to the white table. He tried to sneak his hand under her shirt to touch her belly, but she moved away fast and put some scrambled eggs with bits of green in them on his plate.

'It's tarragon,' she said.

Corbeil is good at catching the feints and hints between lovers, isn't she? She isn't a satirist. That's not her métier. But she can be richly comic. Here's Pullwarden the critic interviewing Allan the actor:

'You were,' Pullwarden says, looking out the front window at the painted brick houses across the road, 'very good in that dog thing. Not a very good play, but you gave a lambent performance. The friend I was with at the time was very taken. We all were.'

'Thank you.'

'Yes, a very vital performance.'

'It was a good experience. I usually hoard myself until there's an audience. It tends to freak out directors who want it right away, you know what I mean. But here, it's the weirdest thing. I got it almost right away, and then working out the bits, it's kind of ... It's just so huge. It requires so much muscle of every kind. It's ...'

'I collect Hamlets, Allan,' Pullwarden interrupts. He is still staring at the brick house across the street. 'And my collection is extensive, it dates back twenty years, to when I saw Ian McKellen playing it in Cardiff. I've seen the very greatest, and the not so greats, and the lost. When you see the lost playing it, it's like seeing a horse with dropped reins – whereas you've seen others run with a speech, they're chewing at it like nettles by the side of the road.'

Like all well-observed fools, Pullwarden is immensely oblivious to his own follies. Well, it's easy pickings to finger the pomposity in a critic, some might say, but Corbeil goes beyond that and exhibits the greater, more fatal follies at the heart of Pullwarden and in the process makes him a fool to reckon others against in contemporary fiction. Corbeil is also humorous in a larger-hearted way that's far more difficult to capture with a few lines from here or there: what she tracks and nets through subtle shifts in the tone of their utterances and reflections as one scene is played off against others is the self-mockery that's close to the surface in many of her other characters here and, equally, in *Voice-over*. Its absence makes Pullwarden awful and its presence makes Alice appealing and so much more typical of a Canadian woman who is really good at her job than the female leads in too many of our books.

Corbeil's characters, her younger men no less than her women, force themselves and their lovers out of the wings and into the central dramas of their own lives by taking risks and enduring the harsh illuminations of self-consciousness and then the consciousness beyond self-consciousness that is moral judgement. This is the way that Shakespeare resonates in this novel. Corbeil doesn't do Shakespeare by numbers: the joinery between the tales told in *Hamlet* and those of *In the Wings* aren't made by connecting up traced outlines of plot in direct paraphrases. Corbeil is too subtle a writer and too good a student of Shakespeare for that. By making Allan something less than the fully articulated self-consciousness and genius in expressiveness that is Hamlet and by dozens of smaller strokes, she offers Allan and her other players the opportunity of following Shakespeare's script or their own and because choices are made that both reflect and refract *Hamlet,* the play becomes a thing in which the consciences of a theatre company are captured. For those of us who read Shakespeare as Samuel Johnson did 'the better to enjoy life, or the better to endure it', *In the Wings* is intensely committed to clarifying what is to be enjoyed, what is to be endured and what ought to be altered in the ways we live now. Especially, I'd say, in lust and in love. For me, it's the seriousness and sympathy Corbeil brings to sexual tensions and their resolution that is the freshest and most refreshing mark of her writing. This is the history of sexual tensions between Allan and Kristen:

The first time Allan ever saw Kristen, she wore flannel pyjamas and was about to seduce a travelling salesman. Randy Tetrault played the travelling salesman and Allan, who was watching the play from the third row, could feel the pocket of warmth between Kristen's small breasts and the flannel of her pyjamas when Randy put his hand there. He fell in love with her right then and there, fell in love with the idea of sheltering her.

He couldn't get enough of her in the beginning, he kept losing himself in her pale face, her body, her past, her relatives, even her clothes. Kristen wore petticoats and lace-up boots and bits of tartan and leather and sat with her legs wide open. He was enthralled by her, never more so than when she took to confessing her sexual fantasies, most of them not too surprisingly – she was after all an actress – having to do with being watched. She fantasized about doing provocative things behind glass while men masturbated. She said that she would come when they came, she was both man and woman in all her fantasies. Did he think there was something wrong with that?

Nothing, nothing wrong with that, he said, and worshipped her. But as time went on, he noticed that Kristen wasn't really there when they made love. She sent her body as some kind of emissary; it was very removed; she kept her eyes closed, and it felt as if she was imagining herself, not making love to him. And then she stopped wanting sex altogether, and cuddled against him and treated him like a stuffed animal, and took to playing house, and that scared him. Closing off all possibilities of sex scared him.

And here's Alice sorting through her history with Allan:

Midnight. Allan is still out. Alice can't sleep, gets out of bed and goes down to the basement to take laundry out of the dryer, and finds there, commingled in all innocence, her clothes and Allan's. His T-shirts, his jeans, his socks, her underwear, her T-shirts, her socks. Her underwear clinging to his socks in static embrace ...

Now she separates their clothes, while sitting on the carpet in the living-room. His socks are all the same, pale grey with a band of white and red at the top. It makes it easier to match them. She rolls the socks into balls, then smooths a white T-shirt on the carpet, tucks back the short sleeves and folds it into two, picks up the perfect square of white cotton, and buries her face in it.

It is a kind of torment loving him, torment, like having ticks burrowing in every pore. It doesn't matter how much. It doesn't matter how often. She wants him all the time. And she doesn't even want what they have now, she wants what they had in the beginning.

In the beginning she tried to cure herself through excess. It was hard to do this while trying to appear nonchalant. She was so scared of scaring him with her appetites. There was something so virginal about him that she found herself going through the motions of seduction until he was overcome into thinking it was his idea.

She threw herself into his body, but it made no difference how much or how often, nothing ebbed, her appetite never declined. That he could stand intact and impervious, so soon after they made love, seemed like the largest of injustices. He kept his beauty. He kept his heart. Her ribs ached, as if they'd been parted against her will to let out her caged heart. She imagined it, red and pulsing, on the sheets between them.

It has become so difficult to bear – how invisible she is to him – so difficult that she is almost ready to ask him to go.

But it's what lies on the other side of his going that stops her from saying those words, something as dark and as neatly defined as a grave.

What I admire is the way Corbeil has found to describe the intimacies between lovers in her work without being exploitative. It looks easy until you try it, try to show in words how sex can affect the whole of a life and do it in a way that elicits sympathy for both lovers simultaneously without canting or becoming corny. And can you imagine how this woman acts out Queen Gertrude to that man's Hamlet? Carole Corbeil can and does so splendidly that she casts some new light on that old play.

Because I believe no less than Carole Corbeil that the spirits of the dead can be present to the living, I feel D.H. Lawrence – the Lawrence who was a great artist, not the man weakened almost to savagery by chronic illnesses and poverty and the messes in his own marital life – looking over my shoulder at the passage I've quoted and prickling with pleasure at a writer so successfully capturing the life of this woman in love. It's not often that my long-time companion and I read the same novel in the same week, but Ann was eager for me to pick up *In the*

Wings as soon as she had put it down, and I did. When I'd finished it the next day, she asked, 'Wouldn't you say that this is as good as anything being written anywhere?' Indeed I would and I do.

At Lake Balaton, 1954

She'll Always Have Paris

Mavis Gallant is one of the great short story writers of our time.
— Michael Ondaatje

Alice Munro is our Chekhov.
— Cynthia Ozick

This is what is said of Mavis Gallant's 1993 story collection *Across the Bridge* in *Books of the Century: A Hundred Years of Authors, Ideas and Literature from The New York Times*:

> The world Mavis Gallant creates in these 11 stories is urban (mostly Paris or Montreal), deeply conservative and, for all its urbanity, old-fashioned. In the title story, timeless as a fairy tale, everything is stock – except the writing. The material is a staple of popular romantic fiction, which Mrs Gallant subverts with intelligence and wit. Not every story here is that successful. This writer is a scalpel-sharp anatomist of stupidity, and while this skill can make her work very funny, occasionally her humour works at the expense of her characters. But she has few equals. One story here, 'Forain', is as close to perfection as possible, a marvel of wit, feeling and tact in which each detail is exact and telling. That and the title story alone would make this book one of the best collections of fiction in years.

If recognition of literary merit in Canada is measured by Governor General's Awards, *Across the Bridge* was inadequately recognized at home – the 1993 award went to Carol Shields for *The Stone Diaries*. Mavis Gallant, however, was made a Companion of the Order of Canada that year and given a tribute at the International Festival of Authors at Harbourfront before being awarded an honorary doctorate by the University of Toronto the following year. She is not without honours in this country but recognition was slow, halting, and remains too limited and grudging.

Mavis Gallant had been a regular contributor to *The New Yorker* for over twenty years and had published two novels and three collections of stories elsewhere before a Canadian publisher became interested in her in 1973. Critical response to her work was isolated and fragmentary until 1978 when the under-appreciated Geoff Hancock devoted all of issue number 28 of *Canadian Fiction Magazine* to a symposium of her work. In 1996, the omnibus publication of fifty-two stories she has selected herself (together with her preface, which says more in fewer words with greater accuracy about her art than any of the three existing book-length studies I've seen so far) under the title *Selected Stories* in Canada and *Collected Stories* in America brings her achievements into sharper focus. This is what is said of *Collected Stories* in *Books of the Century* a few pages after the entry on *Across the Bridge*:

This 887-page volume of stories written over half a century reveals clearly what an ambitious and accomplished anomaly Mavis Gallant is. An expatriate in spirit long before she left her native Montreal for Paris in 1950, she is fascinated by the modern displaced citizen of an ever more mobile world. Her characters do not flee home; they start out homeless, spending their lives conniving at accommodation with a century that started in horror and is ending in hollowness. As they discover that history does not mean continuity, they draw readers irresistibly into their own myopic quests for a reliable perspective on life. Mrs Gallant primes us to expect them to be good or bad, but never hints which are which; and in her stories tragedy can turn to comedy in a sentence. Except for a satiric streak that has grown more explicit recently, her style, amazingly versatile from the start, has changed little. But she has radically reshaped the short story decade after decade; some of the newer stories are accordions, interlinked tales that suggest a new novelistic mutant. In a real sense her style and her attitude are her message. Her disregard of tight plot and momentum make up her theme: our destiny is to wander, misinterpreting as we go along – just as she has dared to drift in a disorienting century, trusting to her own imaginative compass. It has been a great trip.

Rereading the stories that Mavis Gallant arranged according to when they're set rather than by date of publication, I can't say for certain which was the first I'd ever read or precisely when I read it. At the time of my father's sudden death on January 7th, 1958, and for some time thereafter, gifts came into our house from kind neighbours. One that kept coming for a long time was back issues of *The New Yorker* that were passed along to us (when he knew my taste for it) by our neighbour Mr Coupal, an elderly man who once shook off the lethargy that overcame him each year after his farm's crops had been harvested and with a lovely mixture of shyness and pride showed me a group photograph of the first men enlisted to fly airplanes for the British and Canadian forces in the Great War. Mr Coupal was one of those pilots. He told me he'd become a flier after his career as a salesman of Canadian-made harvesting equipment to Hungary had been terminated by the hostilities. The world of my childhood on Angus Crescent in Regina, Saskatchewan, was surprisingly rich in such people – aliens in an alien land who in their efforts to bend it to their own purposes became as fiercely taciturn as lions so as not to be bent further out of shape by those great efforts and scant rewards. I suspect I was the only one in our house to do more with *The New Yorker* than laugh at the cartoons and look at the advertisements that celebrated styles of living so far beyond the reach of my family as to seem the stuff of fables: I read most of each issue every week. I did not read them well. I read them as fairy tales for the man I thought I'd become so suddenly at thirteen.

Canada in the days of my childhood and adolescence was a fearful place. Even those with two parents were anxious, despite having far greater economic security than my mother could ever hope to provide her family with her immense industry and amazing dexterity with scissors, needles and thread. I mean that fearfulness literally: Canadians were kept in a state of fear and anxiety by big-business interests that grew fatter and fatter, demonizing anything and everything that spoke to any real sense of social and individual purpose. Communism! Communism! Communism! What a rallying cry! And, oh, how often and how shrilly it was heard, especially in CCF-run Saskatchewan where even T.C. Douglas's common-sense socialism was too much a threat to bankers and their pals. And, oh, how the generality of us furthered the corporate bosses and the Liberal and Progressive Conservative frontmen of their purposes, unhappily denigrating, disparaging and just doing-down any symptom of larger awareness in everyone and everything. Who do you think you are? You are nothing if you are not one of us in each and every particular: Conform! Conform! Conform! Buy! Buy! Buy! And because I could thicken my skin to more of this than many others I knew, I've never resented those who left Canada to find their purpose in more enlightened places where not everything was for sale at so cheap a price.

Reading *The New Yorker*, I scarcely noticed the names of writers whose stories I read but from those days to now I've carried in my head the opening lines of one story that wasn't as far removed from the reality of my family life as others. 'In Madrid, nine years ago, we lived on the thought of money. Our friendships were nourished with talk of money we expected to have, and what we intended to do when it came.' Much of the time, I've remembered these two sentences only in the abbreviated form of 'we lived on the thought of money' – six words that sum up an experience of the world of poverty I've always resisted re-entering. Those two sentences in their completeness and finality are the first two sentences of Mavis Gallant's 'When We Were Nearly Young' and it was published in *The New Yorker* in 1960.

The unnamed narrator of Mavis Gallant's 'When We Were Nearly Young' is forced to sell her clothes to gypsies in the flea market of Madrid. She's like enough in age and experiences to her author that it's easy to read this story as a quasi-memoir. I don't think any harm comes from doing so. After the two sentences quoted above, it continues:

> There were four of us – two men and two girls. The men, Pablo and Carlos, were cousins. Pilar was a relation of theirs. I was not Spanish and not a relation, and a friend almost by mistake. The thing we had in common was that we were all waiting for money.... In those days I was always looking for signs. I saw signs in cigarette smoke, in the way ash fell, and in the cards ... I thought these signs – the ash, the smoke, and so on – would tell me what direction my life was going to take and what might happen from now on.

When the money she's expecting doesn't come, she sells her clothes. She

refuses to escape into nineteenth-century romantic fictions by partici-
pating in the games of make-believe the others play:

> It *is* the twentieth century ...
>
> I can hear myself saying grandly, 'I don't want your silly fairy
> tales. I'm trying to get rid of my own.'
>
> Carlos says, 'I've known people like you before. You think you
> can get rid of all the baggage – religion, politics, ideas, everything.
> Well, you won't.'
>
> The other two yawn, quite rightly. Carlos and I are bores....
> Poverty is not a goad but a paralysis ... I could not for the life of
> me have put my nose in a book.... My choice in coming here had
> been deliberate: I had a plan. My own character seemed to me ill-
> defined; I believed that this was unfortunate and unique. I
> thought that if I set myself against a background into which I
> could not possibly merge, some outline would present itself. But
> it hadn't succeeded, because I adapted too quickly. In no time at
> all, I had the speech and the movements and the very expression
> on my face of seedy Madrid.... My financial condition spoke for
> itself. It was like Orwell, in Paris, revelling in his bedbugs.

Money arrives for her finally and she buys white bread and 'three
roasted chickens plus a pound of sweet butter and two three-litre bottles
of white Valdepeñas ... some nougat and chestnut paste'. There's a
quarrel over this dinner and she realizes that her good fortune has made
her an outcast to their society. She leaves Madrid. She goes where and
does what? The story concludes with these words:

> I don't know what became of them, or what they were like when
> their thirtieth year came. I left Madrid. I wrote, for a time, but
> they never answered. Eventually they were caught, for me, not by
> time but by the freezing of memory. And when I looked in the
> diary I had kept during that period, all I could find was descrip-
> tions of the weather.'

It *is* the twentieth century and she is a North American in continental
Europe. Such women are not so bound by necessity to husbands and

specific communities. Such women are freer to act for themselves. Self-knowledge is still a question of learning to discriminate between the genuine and the false – 'I don't want your silly fairy tales. I'm trying to get rid of my own.' And the opposition is always a Carlos somewhere saying – 'I've known people like you before. You think you can get rid of all the baggage – religion, politics, ideas, everything. Well, you won't.'

Well, Mavis Gallant did rid herself of many things. As she tells us in her preface to the *Selected Stories*:

> No city in the world drew me as strongly as Paris. (When I am asked why, I am unable to say.) It was a place where I had no friends, no connections, no possibility of finding employment should it be necessary – although, as I reasoned things, if I was to go there with a job and salary in mind, I might as well stay where I was – and where I might run out of money. That I might not survive at all, that I might have to be rescued from deep water and ignominiously shipped home, never entered my head. I believed that if I was to call myself a writer, I should live on writing. If I could not live on it, even simply, I should destroy every scrap, every trace, every notebook, and live some other way. Whatever happened, I would not enter my thirties as a journalist – with stories piling up in a picnic hamper.

Earlier in the preface she notes parenthetically that her six years spent on a Montreal weekly newspaper – the *Standard* – taught her that:

> The distinction between journalism and fiction is the difference between without and within. Journalism recounts as exactly and economically as possible the weather in the street; fiction takes no notice of that particular weather but brings to life a distillation of all weathers, a climate of the mind.

She sold a story to *The New Yorker* and they asked for others and she moved to Paris and that magazine in the person of its great fiction editor William Maxwell kept asking for more stories for a full twenty-five years – all but one of her *Selected Stories* first appeared in *The New Yorker*.

When William Maxwell retired, she was, as she writes, 'inherited by a much younger editor, Daniel Menaker, whom he [Maxwell] liked, trusted, and chose.' It was a brilliant choice. Daniel Menaker has encouraged her gifts for comedy and satire – elements that I don't think work at the expense of her characters, whatever the *New York Times* might say. Mavis Gallant is, as they rightly state, a 'scalpel-sharp anatomist of stupidity' who I'd say is a match for George Eliot. Both can and do upend conventions and subvert them with wit that owes more to deep intelligence than toffee-nosed cleverness. The great difference between them is that Mavis Gallant can do it in the tight compass that's required more often by a twentieth-century magazine than a nineteenth-century one. She can turn character and mood around on the dime of a sentence rather than the old penny of a full paragraph.

Mavis Gallant begins her preface to the stories with the 'hopeless question' that journalists so like to pose, 'Why do you write?' She cites answers from Samuel Beckett, Georges Bernanos, Colette, Marguerite Yourcenar, Jean-Paul Sartre and then ends her opening paragraph with Aleksander Wat telling her 'that it was like the story of the camel and the Bedouin; in the end, the camel takes over. So that was the writing life: an insistent camel.'

She sums up the feeding habits of that camel she has become in three brilliant paragraphs. This is the first of them:

The first flash of fiction arrives without words. It consists of a fixed image, like a slide or (closer still) a freeze frame, showing characters in a simple situation. For example, Barbara, Alec, and their three children, seen getting down from a train in the south of France, announced 'the Remission.' The scene does not appear in the story but remains like an old snapshot or a picture in a newspaper, with a caption giving all the names. The quick arrival and departure of the silent image can be likened to the first moments of a play, before anything is said. The difference is that the characters in the frame are not seen, but envisioned, and do not have to speak to be explained. Every character comes into being with a name (which I may change), an age, a nationality, a profession, a particular voice and accent, a family background, a personal history, a destination, qualities, secrets, an attitude toward love, ambition, money, religion, and a private centre of gravity.

At the end of the third paragraph, she writes:

Sometimes, hardly ever, I have seen clearly that a character sent from nowhere is standing in for someone I once knew, disguised as thoroughly as a stranger in a dream. I have always let it stand. Everything I start glides into print, in time, and becomes like a house once lived in.

It's with this in mind and this sense of 'a house once lived in' that I call 'When We Were Nearly Young' a quasi-memoir and don't think any harm comes from doing so. When Carlos says to the unnamed narrator, 'I've known people like you before. You think you can get rid of all the baggage – religion, politics, ideas, everything. Well, you won't,' I don't know if he is saying something that was ever said to the young writer Mavis Gallant once lived inside but those words have long seemed to me to sum up the artistic code (not the personal one) of her fiction writing. In her stories, it's the religion, the politics, the ideas, the 'everything' of the characters and not Mavis Gallant's personal 'baggage' that controls characters and actions. By using the approach she favours in her fiction, she's making a political decision – the same one found in the great Italian neo-realist films *The Bicycle Thief, Miracle in Milan, Umberto D* or, for that matter, the humanism of the Italian Renaissance. It's poised between and equally opposed to any and all ideologies of individualism and collectivism on the one side and the propaganda of socialist realism and capitalist idealism on the other. Her approach is documentary, almost ethnological (except that it's far more intellectually and morally independent than any ethnologist is ever likely to be) and it reminds readers who remember life before television that Mavis Gallant's six years at the *Standard* correspond to the last years of the golden era of photo journalism.

Gabor Szilasi's photograph of a young man and woman in bathing suits on a motorcycle at Lake Balaton in Hungary in 1954 with the riders in sharp focus and the other bathers in a blur in the background – the image that was used to advertise *Gabor Szilasi, photographs 1954–1996* at the Montreal Museum of Fine Arts in 1997 – is the precise physical equivalent of Mavis Gallant's 'freeze frame'. The field of photography has undergone more immense economic, technical, and theoretical revolutions than literature in the decades Gabor Szilasi has been taking pictures and Mavis Gallant has been writing stories. Gabor sometimes uses 35mm cameras of far greater technical precision than the Zorkig, the old Russian copy of a Leica, that he employed for his motorcycle riders, but most of his images have been made with a large-format camera. Such a camera doesn't leave much room for spontaneity but it allows great precision and tremendous control of the image and establishes a high degree of complicity between the photographer and the photographed. It makes contact rather than snoops: it incorporates more signs of social position and way of life as significant elements than smaller, tighter frames. The images a large-format camera produces only look old-fashioned and lacking in technical sophistication to those for whom the newest wave of anything is the only edge worth contemplating. Gabor Szilasi's photographs are anomalies that stand oddly angled to the real and outside fashion. The same can be said of Mavis Gallant's stories.

Reflecting on fifty years of constant gestation, Mavis Gallant tells us that:

I keep the sketchiest sort of files, few letters and almost no records. As it turned out, I had published more stories than I had expected. This is a heavy volume, and if I had included everything, even nearly everything, it would have become one of those tomes that can't be read in comfort and that are no good for anything except as a weight on sliced cucumbers. I rejected straight humour and satire, which dates quickly, seven stories that were pieces of novels, stories that seemed to me not worth reprinting, stories that I was tired of, and stories that bored me. I also removed more than a dozen stories that stood up to time but not to the practical requirements I've mentioned. Their inclusion would have made this collection as long as the *Concise Oxford* to 'speedometer,' or the whole of *The Oxford Book of American Verse* plus some of the *Oxford English*, as far as Sir Thomas Wyatt, or the King James Bible from Genesis to about the middle of Paul's first Epistle to the Romans.

I would be happy to forgo comfortable reading for such a comprehensive volume, but even though it's a full dozen tales short of completeness in terms of all her most outstanding work, *The Selected Stories* does eliminate a difficulty I've faced whenever anyone has asked where to start reading when it comes to Mavis Gallant. And it supplies me with a more satisfactory answer to that other impossible question that journalists like to ask, the desert island question, as in 'What three books would you take with you if you were to be marooned on a desert island?'

Until *The Selected Stories* came along, I've always been quick to recommend the book of hers I treasure most highly, the 1979 collection *From the Fifteenth District*, because it contains 'The Moslem Wife', 'The Remission', the title story itself and the single story I admire most in all her work – 'Baum, Gabriel, 1935– ( ) '. During a visit to Montreal in September 1998, this is what Mavis Gallant had to say about that story while being interviewed by Ian McGillis for the Montreal *Gazette*.

[McGillis:] Picking highlights from such a uniformly excellent oeuvre is a purely subjective exercise, but for this reader, 'Baum, Gabriel, 1935– ( )' springs to mind. It's a story covering a quarter-century in the life of the orphaned Gabriel and his German friend, Dieter, as they eke out a living as bit actors in war films being shot in postwar Paris. The seldom-attempted theme of male friendship is handled beautifully, and though the scenario of a German and a Jew playing characters who could have been their real-life enemies risks leaden symbolism, it does not weigh the story down for a moment.

[Gallant:] That is one I do like, but nobody ever mentions it. What that story really is is Montparnasse through several decades. I'm glad you like it, because it's one that I think worked, and I don't always think that. It's interesting that you see it as the story of friendship between two men, because that hadn't occurred to me. I think of it as a social history. I never actually use the word Jew, for example, because that would have pulled it over into another Holocaust thing, so I left it open. Oh, you've given me the greatest possible pleasure by liking that one.

[McGillis:] Another story that stands out, this time by venturing into the realm of the fantastic, is 'From the Fifteenth District', in which ghosts complain of being harassed by the living.

[Gallant:] I got the idea for that one from hearing widows of poets and so on, saying 'Of course, he absolutely adored me, he couldn't write his poetry unless I was there.' I remember thinking, what if these people could come back to life, and say 'Stop haunting me with these lies'.

Ian McGillis seems to me a writer worth watching, especially after he gains enough self-confidence to both think and say that picking highlights isn't a purely subjective exercise as long as we share in a common language that is greater in genius than the uses any of us make of it. McGillis is smart – not only smart enough to get Mavis Gallant to comment with useful insights into two splendid stories, but smart enough to ask her where she was when France won the World Cup:

[Gallant:] Oh, that was wonderful ... I wouldn't have left for any-thing. There were 60-something matches and I saw at least a bit of each one.... The night they won, I wanted to go to the Champs-Elysées, but I couldn't get a single friend to go with me. I was afraid to go alone because I had broken two toes, and I thought someone might step on my foot.

That comes just after McGillis has elicited a comment from her on the change in reception she's had in Canada over the years from utter obscurity to her current celebrity status:

Well, my work was completely unknown here for years. I was in *The New Yorker*, and this was an era of strong Canadian nationalist feelings. Anyone who didn't live in Canada was considered a kind of traitor, and I couldn't be bothered even considering that.

The hell with it. It was the early 80s before that began to change, but even then, I remember coming to Toronto and taking a lot of guff from writers: 'While we were here, pulling culture up by the bootstraps, some people were sitting in cafés.' I remember someone saying that.

83

Choose as you like. And just as we don't have to choose only one of her stories – even 'Baum, Gabriel, 1935– ( )' – to the exclusion of all others, no one has to choose to read Mavis Gallant to the exclusion of reading Alice Munro. I don't know anyone who has read Mavis Gallant who would do such a thing but, unfortunately, I have come across any number of readers who do the reverse, who tell me, 'After reading Alice Munro, I won't read anybody else's stories.'

Alice Munro does inspire a queer fanaticism bordering on loyalty among some of her readers. I don't blame her for it, not for an instant. Most writers don't get the readers they most deserve and I sometimes wonder if Alice Munro wouldn't happily swap whole gaggles of her true believers for a few more with ears perfectly pitched to the rhythms of her prose and minds that don't decompress when they dive into the depths of her intelligence. All I know about Prof. David Staines's mind and ear is that he's the general editor of the New Canadian Library, an erstwhile Giller Prize juror, and an occasional guest on various C B C radio programs where he likes to display a true fanatic's zeal and minute knowledge of Broadway musicals (a predilection I think might just be God's way of telling people they've got too much free time on their hands). Whatever else he knows and does, Professor Staines did seem to me to go as far over the top as Ethel Merman in his verbal hanging, drawing and quartering of the 1998 Governor General's Awards fiction jurors for not shortlisting Alice Munro's *Love of a Good Woman*. Why was she passed over? *Quill & Quire* put two questions to the jurors and published the replies in its January 1999 issue. The first question was, 'In your opinion, why was Alice Munro's *The Love of a Good Woman* not one of the best books of the year?'

David Arnason said, 'It was lacking a freshness, an imaginative force, all those kinds of things that make a book really interesting. If you're an Alice Munro fan, I'm sure everything in there you'll love. I like Alice Munro, I think she's a fine writer, but I'm not a true believer.'

Eric McCormack said, 'I had trouble getting through Alice Munro. I read all the stories very carefully, and found some really, really tedious. You can't give a prize to something tedious. There are books by her I've really enjoyed – but this wasn't one of them. It was very mundane. I mean, that's what she does, but this was the mundane done in a mundane way.'

Susan Swan said, 'I've been astounded. People act as if I'm against her. I think she should have the Nobel Prize. I always felt Staines was right to criticize us for leaving Munro off, but had been upset by his comment that there was no major work on our list. There is enough good stuff for two shortlists in Canada.'

Quill & Quire's second question was, 'Is the Governor General's Award for fiction purely about choosing the best work of fiction in Canada that year?'

David Arnason said, 'Three people acting in good faith, absolutely honestly, made what trade-offs they had to in order to choose between them the five best books in the country. It was based on what the book accomplished, not on reputation or anything else.'

Eric McCormack said, 'It's idiotic to think that there are five objective best. You have to contend with the particular tastes of the jury assembled. We each chose ten books. There was overlap, but there was one book I couldn't get anyone to go for. For me it was one of the greatest reads, but the other two judges wouldn't be persuaded.'

Susan Swan said, 'It's the five best books as far as this jury is concerned. You're a citizen of that committee and you have to deal with what the citizens of the jury want. It's a subjective, informed, literary opinion. I did go in intending to pick what I thought was the best book, but I also wanted to recognize newer faces. That was one of my aspirations. The other was literary excellence.'

All of that is fairly said. Their shortlist was a very good one: here it is with the jury citations as released to the press by the Canada Council.

ENGLISH-LANGUAGE NOMINEES / FICTION

Lynn Coady, Vancouver –
Strange Heaven (Goose Lane Editions)
Lynn Coady's *Strange Heaven* is a lively and fascinating glimpse of a young woman's life in the Maritimes and her relationship to her family. At play is the whole range of emotional possibility, from sharp comedy to pathos. This is fresh, energetic writing with a distinctive and individual voice.

Barbara Gowdy, Toronto –
The White Bone (Harper Flamingo Canada/HarperCollins)
An original, imaginative achievement which challenges our perceptions of the role of animals in the making of culture. Gowdy's evocation of the rich emotional and intellectual life of a herd of elephants astounds, delights and ultimately convinces.

Wayne Johnston, Toronto –
The Colony of Unrequited Dreams (Alfred A. Knopf Canada)
Wayne Johnston's *The Colony of Unrequited Dreams* is a powerful act of imagination. It captures the whole sweep of Newfoundland history and contains it in a story that is personal, moving and funny. It does for Newfoundland what Dostoyevsky did for Russia. It is filled with wonderful characters and creates a vivid and intrinsic sense of what it means to be a Newfoundlander.

Kerri Sakamoto, Toronto –
The Electrical Field (Alfred A. Knopf Canada)
This is an eerie novel. A murder mystery set in southern Ontario among a group of Japanese Canadians. Enigmatic and delightful, Kerri Sakamoto's writing sizzles with energy.

Diane Schoemperlen, Kingston, Ontario –
Forms of Devotion (A Phyllis Bruce Book/HarperCollins)
An elegant collection of stories. Diane Schoemperlen's writing is uncommonly wise and full of a sense of wonder. The wood engravings and line drawings add depth and richness to the text.

And the winner with the jury's citation was,

Diane Schoemperlen, Kingston, Ontario –
Forms of Devotion (A Phyllis Bruce Book/HarperCollins)
A witty and brilliant collection of stories. The author's delicate, playful approach to faith or the lack of it in our lives is the work of a major literary talent at the top of her craft. A virtuoso performance. The elegant and scintillating writing in this collection is enriched by the selection of wood engravings and line drawings from earlier centuries. A book that can be read and reread many times for pleasure and stimulation.

Like most of the Giller Prize jurors, past and present, David Staines is a McClelland & Stewart loyalist and I suppose he was pissed off that no writer from that press was on the list. I don't know how else to explain his denigration of Barbara Gowdy's and Wayne Johnston's novels as something less than major works. The Giller jury of Margaret Atwood, Peter Gzowski and Guy Vanderhaeghe obviously thought otherwise by including both of them on their shortlist together with *The Healer*, by Greg Hollingshead, *A Recipe for Bees*, by Gail Anderson-Dargatz, and their winner, *The Love of a Good Woman*, by Alice Munro.

Barbara Gowdy, Wayne Johnston and Diane Schoemperlen are three of the most interesting and accomplished fiction writers in North America today. They're not minor leaguers in any sense and all three of their books mark out new and very promising directions in their work. For me, to choose one among them in preference to the other two would not be an easy thing because each is distinguished and utterly distinct from the others. Diane Schoemperlen is quite likely the best student Alice Munro has ever had. Writing in the September 1998 issue of *Books in Canada*, Nikki Abraham opens her review of *Forms of Devotion* with this observation:

You know how a really great jazz musician can take an old tune and play with it – twist it, bend it, loop it back on itself, turn it upside down, appear to abandon it completely and then, with a sly flourish, return it to you fresh, new, still itself but transformed now into a thing with possibilities instead of something to be listened to with the mind on hold? That's what Diane Schoemperlen does for the short story.

To take that thought and develop it further and more precisely, Diane Schoemperlen is to Alice Munro and Alice Munro is to the American large-circulation-magazine short story as Oscar Peterson is to Art Tatum and Art Tatum is to the Broadway show song. Take Schoemperlen's 'Body Language' for instance: a man is in love with his wife but can't stop her drifting away from him. It's a tale not untold by Alice Munro. Schoemperlen's treatment is indebted to any one of Munro's in pretty much the way that Peterson's playing of a Gershwin tune is indebted to Tatum's. Each is an original. I can easily imagine Alice Munro in the full maturity of her writing career absolutely delighted to see Diane Schoemperlen in mid-career rewarded in her sixth book with a Governor General's Award for writing stories that continue Alice Munro's own sense of story with surprising coun- terpoints and sly variations: Alice Munro understands better than most of us what it is to stand within a tradition.

Cynthia Ozick, who never gets these things wrong in her essays and reviews, has written of Alice Munro, 'She is our Chekhov.' As writer and critic, Cynthia Ozick has a surer grasp of more aspects of the short story than I'm ever likely to comprehend. This isn't false modesty: Cynthia Ozick is a genius and part of her genius lies in being able to trace things that most of us on this side of the Atlantic think of as peculiarly North American back to their European roots and often further into their relatedness to Talmudic Judaism. For myself, I've always seen Alice Munro in continuity with William Maxwell and not much else. Mavis Gallant says of William Maxwell, 'I owe him everything,' and Alice Munro said much the same when she paid tribute to him on CBC Radio some years ago.

I'd very much like to see Mavis Gallant become the first Canadian winner of the Nobel Prize for literature (yes, I do know Saul Bellow was born here) but I doubt it's going to happen: she doesn't have enough true believers in the Canadian academic community to lobby on her behalf. But whatever happens or fails to happen in Sweden, Mavis Gal- lant will still have Paris – a half century and more of life there. That's more and better than Ingrid Bergman gets at the end of *Casablanca*.

Whenever I talk casually with those who were here in Canada 'pulling culture up by the bootstraps', it's amazing how many Hollywood films and Broadway songs get discussed with such exquisite attention to fine detail: truly, this is the country of Trivial Pursuit. Those who talk so easily of American pop culture always make me wonder if it's not a shorter distance to the heart of Canadian identity and experience from a café in Paris than from a movie theatre on the Bloor-Yonge corridor. Then again, I suspect Mavis Gallant has never spent much time in cafés. Remember what they said of Hemingway in his Paris years? Nobody ever saw him unless he really wanted to be seen — he was too busy writing as well as he could. There's something to be said for the way living in a city of light and enlightenment pushes an artist to achieve greatness or be crushed. Mavis Gallant is an artist and a great one, one of the great storytellers of all time, a George Eliot in our time.

Mordecai Richler, 1973

There's a Purple Dinosaur in My Doghouse

> ... the true function of a writer is to produce a masterpiece ... no other function is of any consequence.
>
> — Cyril Connolly

> I've never known a writer or painter anywhere who wasn't a self-promoter, a braggart, and a paid liar or a coward, driven by avarice and desperate for fame.
>
> — Barney Panofsky in *Barney's Version.*

Mordecai Richler is more of a hedgehog than a fox. I don't mean his legendary prickliness – that's a consequence. I mean what Isaiah Berlin meant when he popularized this mildly fatuous distinction between two kinds of thinker that was first made by an ancient Greek poet. Richler is single-minded: he's known a few big things throughout his life as a writer and never tires of pursuing them. He is a conservative moralist who writes from the standpoint of values that are increasingly ignored or mocked by the subsets of society he condemns. In order to honour what is good, he condemns whatever is ignorant and silly and self-serving. Growing up in the Saint Urbain district of Montreal in the forties and early fifties and taking the interest he took in boxing, baseball, hockey and novel-writing, Richler perceived with great clarity that there must be moral and not merely idiosyncratic differences between those who play in the big leagues and bush-leaguers. 'Style is morality' wrote Cyril Connolly. When you make it to the top, when you've mastered a truly difficult skill in such a way that you're an artist in a world of craftsmen, when you're Muhammad Ali, Jackie Robinson, Wayne Gretzky or Mordecai Richler, you've got a responsibility to hold that higher ground. Not just against other contenders, not really. First of all, last of all, most of all, you can't surrender an inch to any pretender. Richler has made a career out of slapping flyweights down. He can't resist doing so even in circumstances that sometimes leave others scratching their heads. Richler's sarcastic jabs, uppercuts and right hooks have been so anathema for so long among so many in both *haut-bourgeois* and *rive-gauche* Montreal that I'm disconcerted whenever I don't need to immediately leap to his defence. I've been disconcerted a lot lately by the *haute-bourgeoisie.*

Barney's Version is a great success and Richler has never been so popular in the upper west end of his home town, to judge from the comments I hear on the mid-level of Westmount where I live and where the *demitasse bourgeoisie* drink their espresso diluted with a lot of water and milk: *allongé, s'il vous plaît* as they say on the terrasse of the *pâtisserie* around the corner from our flat. So it's not surprising to me that the most extravagant literary estimate of *Barney's Version* emanates from a scion of one of the haughtier households. In a very lengthy review essay 'Richler's Paradise Lost' in the November 1997 *Books in Canada,* Scott Disher who used to call himself I. Scott Disher, as if he might possibly be mistaken for anyone but himself, writes:

> His creative powers undiminished, Richler has survived the indignities of time and controversy. He is unquestionably this country's most celebrated male novelist. Neither his stature abroad, however, nor his literary seniority here will shield him from a predictable rash of indignant and venomous responses to a novel that revels in provocation. *Barney's Version* is a personal paean that delights in skewering and roasting the self-righteous advocates of postmodern moral relativism. If it turns out to be a sort of swan song, Richler and his admirers can take satisfaction in knowing that his tenth novel at last provides its ambitious author entrée into an august literary coterie. Delivered as a *fin-de-siècle* peroration, *Barney's Version* is embroidered with the savage mischief and gleeful scorn of Waugh and the downward spiralling grotesquerie of Bellow's self-destructive anti-heroes.

Disher, a very large man who is very nearly as overstuffed with words as bunched together as a cheap paperback thesaurus's and who appears to have never met an entrée he didn't like, wasn't much of a prophet in his prediction of what sort of response the book was going to get. Richler's novels have rarely been greeted with indignation or venom in recent

years: unlike his essays, his fiction tends to be *safely* reviewed. That isn't
Disher's only mistake as a critic. Richler has been in 'an august coterie'
for a good many years, roughly ever since the publication of *St Urbain's
Horseman* in 1971 established him – abroad if not at home – as the
author of one of the very best novels written in English this half-century.
I'd also say that *Barney's Version* might have things in common with
Waugh's and Bellow's ruder writings but little in common with what
most readers find best in them. But Disher does inadvertently put his
thumbprint on a couple of the principal reasons why *Barney's Version*
has become so well liked by so many. He suggests that to measure the
accomplishments of *Barney's Version* 'one might compare it with other
recent works by prominent novelists pursuing similar things: John
Updike's finale of Harry Angstrom's life, *Rabbit at Rest*, Martin Amis's
The Information, and Richard Ford's second look at the sportswriter
manqué Frank Bascombe in *Independence Day*.' Indeed one might and
Disher does just that, in terms such as these:

> Though perhaps out-of-date, the choice of having a narrator
> commit himself to print provides an authenticity – what the
> French call robustesse – lacking in Updike's and Ford's use of high
> realism's gauzy transcript, which always begs questions: Who is
> the narrator and why? And should the reader have to suffer the
> boredom – verisimilitude is a poor rationale – of being trapped
> from beginning to end, in the stasis of formless, floating thought-
> balloons?

> Unlike Rabbit Angstrom, Barney is truly literate; as for Bas-
> combe, he is a frustrated, self-hating prose man, with an attitude
> towards the fraudulism of literary academia.

> In this novel, Richler's gaudy inventiveness and exuberance
> have been suffused into a seamless but muscular narrative voice,
> minus the languid (self-indulgent) meanderings that Updike and
> Ford lay off on their protagonists as naturalistic narration, a
> stylistic choice that often prompts us to skim and skip. Richler's
> resolutely old-fashioned formulae, faultless mimicry, and
> screenwriter's attention-deficit radar infuse Barney's chaotically

related tale with a rollicking textual interplay, enhanced by clever authorial devices.

After detailing Richler's authorial devices, which are both more (the mimicry) and less (the footnotes, the interior monologues) clever than Disher makes them out to be, he attempts to place *Barney's Version* within Richler's overall accomplishments:

> Throughout his career, Richler and his characters constantly calibrate their progress against the experiences and transformations of peers, real and imagined. The joys and pitfalls of defining and measuring success while striving for its favours are Richler's dominant preoccupation.... We should resist the temptation to simple-mindedly accuse Richler of writing the same book over and over again – a trite ploy often used insultingly of his two great role models, Bellow and Waugh. Instead, readers should see the novels as a process of accretion and exploration. Though arguably another in an assembly-line of maybe-Mordy protagonists, Barney Panofsky is also strikingly similar to Josh Shapiro's sexually irrepressible, alcoholic mother, Esther ...

Then, in his final paragraph, Disher writes:

> Of late, Richler, who is almost comically bad at explaining his motivations and methods, has been repeating a sort of mantra on the book-chat circuit: 'Like every writer, you hope you've done something that will last – and once you've done that, it's time to quit. I don't think I've done that yet.' It's difficult not to view the Book of Barney as a profane testament to a wasted life devoted to trivial pursuits. Certainly, part of this book's sly point-of-view is self-satirical: a send-up of Richler's own tendencies to indulge in ritualistic rants. But I hope that the plethora of abuse hurled at all writers and artists in Barney's sclerotic, envious apologia for himself is not a reflection of the author's own innermost insecurities about the ultimate value of his literary efforts and journalistic diversions.

And, finally, a last quote from earlier in Disher's review so that you can decide, with his assistance, in which categories I ought to be dumped:

> Variously attacked as an ungrateful misanthrope, overpaid Canada-basher, and anti-Francophone bigot, Richler has earned the enmity of a nasty mosaic of Quebec nationalists and their apologists, plus a resentful horde of bizarre bedmates. The anti-Richler brigades stretch from garden-variety anti-Semites and zealots (including Zionists) leftwards across the trendoid spectrum: feministas (and their appeasers), English-Canadian cultural nationalists and their of late less vocal allies, the economic nationalists, anti-Americans, *et al.* As occupant of one of Canada's premier pulpits – a 'sundry ruminations' column in the reconstructed *Saturday Night* – Richler has courted the ire of assorted envious hacks, talking heads, CanLit critics, disheartened socialists, prudes, environmentalists, homophiles, Toronto boosters, bureaucrats and politicians of all persuasions, anti-smoking-cholesterol-alcohol types, and other covens of correctitude.

In sum, for Disher, *Barney's Version* is easy to read, gossipy in nature and naughty towards crude facsimiles of those who mate in beds other than their own. And it's precisely these things that make *Barney's Version* the least of Richler's fictions since *The Incomparable Atuk* of 1963.

Michael Darling, who rates *St Urbain's Horseman* every bit as high as I do, reviewed *Barney's Version* under the title 'Richler Then and Now' in *Canadian Notes & Queries*, Number 52, 1997: 2. For Darling, Barney Panofsky definitely isn't Mordecai Richler. Yes, they are roughly the same age and Jewish Montrealers of the same St Urbain neighbourhood. Barney's world and Richler's world are nearly congruent here as elsewhere in Richler's fiction and Disher is right to find the local up-proppers of Richler's favourite bars in its pages. But Barney has set himself a task Richler will never face: with failing memory and little literary ability, Panofsky is writing a defence of himself against what he takes to be various libels perpetrated against him by a pusillanimous Canadian writer, Terry McIver, who alleges that Barney murdered Bernard (Boogie) Moscovitch, a failed writer of great promise. Yes, for Bernard

Moscovitch you can read the name Mason Hoffenberg, the co-writer of *Candy*. McIver is a catchall and a catcall against arts council-subsidized writers. Barney is a ranter and his storytelling is as motivated by self-justification and desire for revenge as he alleges Terry McIver's to be as he writes down his version of his life with his three wives, his multiple careers and his time in Paris in the fifties.

Darling writes:

> In structure, characterization and theme *Barney's Version* recalls its last three predecessors. Beginning with *Saint Urbain's Horseman*, Richler has adhered to a structure of discontinuous narrative, in which the story is told in seemingly random flashbacks, allowing the major crisis in the protagonist's life to be foregrounded, while all the characters and events that have contributed to it are gradually sketched in so that the background is completed just as the crisis is resolved. Barney's faulty memory is one means of contributing to this design as it allows Richler a psychological motivation for the narrative's abrupt leaps in time and space.

But the key thing, the single factor that places *Barney's Version* at considerable remove from its predecessors, as Darling notes, is that in 'choosing a first-person narrative, Richler actually distances himself from his narrator to a greater degree than if he had stuck with his usual third-person voice.' To prove this point, Darling contrasts a passage from *Barney's Version* and one from *St Urbain's Horseman*. They're so well matched, I have no hesitation in using them again. Here's a typical Panofsky rant:

> Why, in those days we not only used carbon paper, but when you phoned somebody you actually got an answer from a human being on the other end, not an answering machine with a ho ho ho message. In those olden times you didn't have to be a space scientist to manage the gadget that flicked your TV on and off, that ridiculous thingamabob that now comes with twenty push buttons, God knows what for. Doctors made house calls. Rabbis were guys. Kids were raised by their moms instead of in child-care

pens like piglets. Software meant haberdasher. There wasn't a different dentist for gums, molars, fillings, and extractions – one nerd managed the lot. If a waiter spilled hot soup on your date, the manager offered to pay her cleaning bill and sent over drinks, and she didn't sue for a kazillion dollars, claiming 'loss of enjoyment of life'. If the restaurant was Italian it still served something called spaghetti, often with meatballs. It was not yet pasta with smoked salmon, or linguini in all the colours of the rainbow, or penne topped with a vegetarian steaming pile that looked like dog sick. I'm ranting again. Digressing. Sorry about that.

Depending on which side of the bed you got out of this morning, that's more or less diverting – no worse and little better than the things you can pick up on talk radio breakfast shows if your own testosterone is running low and you need a jolt of 'roid rage. It's just a string of clichés, all too utterable. It lacks all of Richler's writerly trademarks. Here's Darling's choice of a representative passage from *St Urbain's Horseman*:

Sitting with the Hershes, day and night, a bottle of Remy Martin parked between his feet, such was Jake's astonishment, commingled with pleasure, in their responses, that he could not properly mourn for his father. He felt cradled, not deprived. He also felt like Rip Van Winkle returned to an innocent and ordered world he had mistakenly believed long extinct. Where God watched over all, doing His sums. Where everything fit. Even the holocaust which, after all, had yielded the state of Israel. Where to say, 'Gentlemen the Queen,' was to offer the obligatory toast to Elizabeth II at an affair, not to begin a discussion on Andy Warhol. Where smack was not habit-forming but what a disrespectful child deserved; pot was what you simmered the chicken soup in; and camp was where you sent the boys for the summer. It was astounding, Jake was incredulous, that after so many years and fevers, after Dachau, after Hiroshima, revolutions, rockets in space, DNA, bestiality in the streets, assassinations in and out of season, there were still brides with shining faces who were married in white gowns, posing for the *Star* social pages with their prizes, pear-shaped boys in evening clothes. There were aunts

who sold raffles and uncles who swore by the *Reader's Digest.*
French Canadians, like overflying airplanes distorting the TV picture, were only tolerated. DO NOT ADJUST YOUR SET, THE
TROUBLE IS TEMPORARY. Aunts still phoned each other every
morning to say what sort of cake they were baking. Who had
passed this exam, who had survived that operation. A scandal was
when a first cousin was invited to the bar mitzvah *kiddush,* but
not the dinner. Eloquence was the rabbi's sermon. They were
ignorant of the arts, they were overdressed, they were overstuffed,
and their taste was appallingly bad. But within their self-
contained world, there was order. It worked.

Like the passage from *Barney's Version,* this too contrasts 'then' and
'now' but look at the differences: Barney simply asserts a litany of
complaints against the idiosyncratic choices of others. Those choices
displease him because they go against his tastes. Fair enough, but none
of it matters unless you share those tastes or care about him as an individual. There's much more at stake in the situation Jake encounters: Jake
is astonished and pleased by an innocence and order in a small part of
the world where everything fits and works in ways that it doesn't in the
larger world. Questions of taste are integral to large issues of morality
and immorality. Here, 'Style is morality': look at how Richler, the
consummate prose stylist, uses balance, parallelism, antithesis and an
artful arrangement of puns to establish rhetorical order! Everything in
the *St Urbain's Horseman* passage asserts that the world might not make
much sense but words can establish the sense of its nonsense. Morality is
human judgement upon the world of men and women and humans
need words to be moral, words that formulate judgements that are balanced, paralleled, antithetical and incarnate beauty, truth and goodness
in as much measure as we can find. Richler here is complex and subtle:
Barney is crude and simple.

Barney is a much clumsier writer and consequently a far clumsier
moralist than Richler. When Richler is on his own game and writing in
his characteristic style, he establishes character through unguarded bits
of dialogue. Nobody does it better. If Richler hadn't shared with Barney
his own pitch-perfect ear for catching the ways people reveal themselves
to one another, *Barney's Version* would be more than half bad. A

random sample: here's Barney describing his second wife coaching him before his first meeting with her parents:

'You are not to order more than one drink at the table before lunch.'

'Right.'

'And whatever you do, no whistling at the table. *Absolutely no whistling at the table.*

'She can't stand it.'

'But I've never whistled at the table in my life.'

Things started badly, Mrs Mock WASP disapproving of our table. 'I should have had my husband make the reservation.'

Sharp, cutting, funny. Another of Richler's great strengths is his ability to shift on the fly from dialogue to interior monologue with a very short throw of words and no double-clutching. Darling gives this example from *St Urbain's Horseman* of a confrontation between Jake Hersh's Gentile wife Nancy and her Jewish mother-in-law. This too is worth repeating not only here but in any lesson on style one writer wants to pass along to another. It's also a very good *aide memoire* to civility in a lot of other situations, say, every time you encounter anyone who's of an age to have survived the Holocaust:

'If you can't eat butter on your salami sandwich,' Nancy charged, unable to contain her tears any more, 'how come you can have eggs with your hot dogs!'

'Eggs are *parve*,' Mrs Hersh returned haughtily.

'Oh! Oh! Oh!' Nancy stamped her foot. She stamped it again. 'Sometimes all your Jewish hocus-pocus –'

Six million isn't enough for them. (My italics)

Richler uses all of six words spoken silently by Mrs Hersh to capture the sheer terror and defence mechanism that surfaces in her at the merest of foot-stampings. Yes, it's ludicrous for Mrs Hersh to feel a threat of persecution in such a situation but for any Jewish woman of a certain age, one of the great lessons of the Holocaust is that no act is too trivial to be the basis of damnation by anti-Semites. It's the morality of the distressed survivor in every age of acute anxiety: reading this, I think immediately of the almost incomprehensible scrupulosity of moral theologians of the latter year of the Middle Ages as they scribbled away specifying the smallest degrees of sin in a world that had lost one-third of its population to the Black Death and its pandemic recurrences – a mid-fourteenth century handbook of instruction for priests lists sins of thought, sins of words and sins of action, including sins against God and neighbour and the seven deadly sins, sins of the senses with various parts of the body (including sins of the head, neck, ears, eyes, nose, mouth, tongue, gullet, hands, stomach, genitals, heart, knees, feet), sins against the twelve articles of faith, sins against the seven sacraments, sins against the seven virtues, sins against the seven gifts of the Holy Spirit, and sins against the eight beatitudes. 'Style is morality.' How odd it is that Richler's genius is so undervalued in a Gentile society whose literary traditions owe much to the brief dialogues and even briefer interior reflections of the Gospels: why anyone raised within earshot of a Bible attaches any moral weight whatsoever to the bloated, orotund language of Robertson Davies baffles me. 'Style is morality.'

Thematically, this very point about style as substance is highlighted through a quotation from Samuel Johnson that Barney cites in support of his admission that he enjoys reading memoirs and biographies that really dish the dirt on celebrities, McIver's notwithstanding:

'If nothing but the bright side of characters should be shown, we should sit down in despondency, and think it utterly impossible to imitate them in *anything*. The sacred writers ... related the vicious as well as the virtuous actions of men; which had this moral effect, that it kept mankind from despair.'

In *St Urbain's Horseman*, Jake also invokes Samuel Johnson but with a world of difference. Speaking to Nancy, he tells his wife that she ought not to be terrified by the potential damage from his trial at the Old Bailey:

Who cares? You, me. It doesn't really matter. You know what's important to me? Really, really important to me? Dr Samuel Johnson. I keep wondering, if I had lived in his time, would he have liked me? Would Dr Johnson have invited me to sit at his table?

Jake has a larger view of redemption than Barney. Jake's includes amendment of life and the favour of Heaven in the form of being seated at a London table as humanly fulfilling as Jesus's own. Barney has utterly given up on anything outside himself, better than himself, except Moscovitch who isn't substantial enough to bear even this small weight. Moscovitch's life is utterly misspent. At Barney's trial for murder, unlike Jake's trial, the central question of the book isn't answered. In Barney's case, the trial becomes little more than an excuse for a few barbs at the Catholic Church's connivance in corruption within Quebec's judicial system. And Barney once more becomes just another ranter whose deeper motives are obscure to himself and whose voice grates on the reader's nerves rather than elicits human sympathy.

Barney's Version is not a step backward, there are no backward steps for an internationally renowned author of 10 novels and numerous other works. But it is an experiment that hasn't quite succeeded.

That's Darling's final sentence and the only false note in his review. It's just silly – there are backward steps for all authors, regardless of renown. And Darling ought to recognize *Barney's Version* as one because he edited *Perspectives on Mordecai Richler* for ECW in 1986 and it contains Wilfred Cude's 'Jacob Hersh, Dr Johnson, and Joseph K.: Literary Allusion and Comic Resolution in *St Urbain's Horseman*', the single best piece of writing about Richler's masterpiece I've encountered.

Cude doesn't make the mistake of an unwary reader by taking Jake Hersh at his own self-valuation as a disappointment to himself and a washout. Cude rightly sees Jake 'as an artist of still-latent but considerable potential and as a genuinely ethical person striving for maturity and grace.' Then Cude does a quite unorthodox and wonderful thing for a literary critic to do in this country, he actually follows the clearly marked trail of Richler's literary allusions in *St Urbain's Horseman* and enters into the comparison between Jake and Dr Johnson that Richler implies. With good reason. Dr Johnson is one of 'those who were truly great, those who come nearest the sun.' Cude builds a powerful case that:

> The parallel between Jacob Hersh and Samuel Johnson is consistent and sustained, serving to emphasize the artistic potential that Jake is about to realize at the novel's conclusion ... Jake accepts Luke's offer to direct his script, an opportunity that will do for him what the *Dictionary* did for Samuel Johnson. Everything has finally come together: a script of unquestionable excellence, a working environment with all the professional resources Luke's established talent guarantees, a return to the close artistic rapport developed so long ago with a friend. Granted, we cannot say for sure whether or not Jake will attain an artistry consistent with his ambitions and dreams. But as we reckon the odds, we should recollect the parallel with bohemian Sam.

In the character of Jake Hersh, Mordecai Richler achieves 'a rather unusual and unprecedented feat, the presentation of a distinguished artist at the moment of moving from obscurity into mature accomplishment in both art and ethics,' Cude goes on to say and I agree. Wholeheartedly. Amen. This is a considerable achievement for any novel but *St Urbain's Horseman* goes well beyond this in its artistic complexity and moral profundity. Nancy, Jake's wife, is a mirror of decency, loyalty and courage but she's Jake's opposite in terms of her ability to casually enjoy social life. Jake, to use the language common at the end of the century, is totally conflicted all the time as he struggles to preserve his own cultural birthright as a Jew. *Pace* the Book of Job and Kafka, Jake's trial at the Old Bailey is a trial within a series of trials. Everything that happens in court is replayed again at home in front of Nancy. Not content with setting the public versus the private, Richler ups the stakes to include Jake's personal history as it intersects with the history of the Jewish people. His trial at the Old Bailey is another in a long series of ensnarlments between Jake and man's laws, his Jewishness and the world. Cude, once more:

> Back and back Jake goes into the foulest recesses of history, trial after trial, war after war, back ever back with his cousin Joseph, plumbing the dark depths that cast shadows of evil into his life.

This is the solemn and awful theme of man's laws and the Law, the central theme of the novel, the one resounding theme that makes this an international classic.

In another good and useful essay in Darling's collection titled 'St Urbain's Horseman: The Novel as Witness', Thomas E. Tausky articulates Richler's wide-ranging knowledge and profound emotional commitment to the Holocaust through an analysis of the sources Richler employs and the precise uses he makes of them. Richler is opposed in principle to any attempt to add fictional elements to the Holocaust story. His detailed descriptions of the death camps in St Urbain's Horseman are based entirely upon factual accounts. Where he turns his fancy loose (and what a wonderful thing it is) is in the comic response he provides to Kafka's tragic question in The Trial. Once again, Cude picks up all of Richler's allusions,

> An answer to Kafka, until now unanticipated in the tradition of international classics, a comic response in English to the tragic vision of Der Prozess. How like and yet unlike these two classics of Jewish literature are. Each with its bewildered and frightened protagonist, a middle class would-be swinger in his thirties, hounded and haunted by his nation's laws and dreading the outcome of his trial. And each with the Trial itself, conducted in baffling and mysterious circumstances, carried out over a number of perverse and convoluted exercises in legal mummery, constituting less a consummation of justice than another refinement in torment.... And yet St. Urbain's Horseman is no mere echo of The Trial, notwithstanding the many broad points of similarity between them, a fact which reinforces the claim of the Canadian work to classic stature.
>
> Though St. Urbain's Horseman looks to the same moral nightmare as The Trial, the artistic stance is totally different, reflected in the selection of the comic rather than the tragic mode. Jacob Hersh is a talented artist venturing forth on his mature achievement, but Joseph K. is a mediocre clerk doomed to die 'like a dog'. St. Urbain's Horseman is a comedy, in Dante's sense of the word, achieving a 'longed for, fortunate and pleasing'

conclusion. *The Trial* is a tragedy, in Aristotle's sense of the word, offering a conclusion inspiring only 'pity and fear'. Both are brilliant morality plays, addressing firmly and frankly the terrifying ethical and spiritual issues of our age; and it is truly remarkable that the tragedy preceded the holocaust, while the comedy came after. Evil, human evil, is considered unflinchingly in both works; and only the artistic perspective changes, leaving the international community now free to choose the vision more suitable to its needs.

The last sentence, admittedly, is a weird one. I don't get around as much as maybe I should but I seriously doubt if visions of either sort are ever freely chosen by international communities of any size or description. Or is this what members of International Societies for the Study of Post- and Post-Post do when David Lodge isn't watching? Then again, I don't know Kafka the way Cude does – at least as well as Richler knows *The Trial*.

Cude's list of similarities between Kafka's trial scenes and Richler's includes 'intensified sexuality, ritual flagellation, symbolic portraiture, pessimistic co-defendants, even a confused reading of a latter-day political parable, the fragment of a parody filmscript, all festering together in a dark and stultifying legal atmosphere generated by incessant falsehood.' All the falsehoods notwithstanding, the English-speaking justice of the Old Bailey does work: Jake is reprimanded and fined £500 and costs. Cude, in his summation, finds:

> This is Dante's pleasing conclusion: pleasing artistically, since it is consistent with the overall development of the texts; pleasing ethically since it is consistent with the fundamental innocence of the protagonist; and pleasing intellectually, since it points the way to a viable resolution of all those endlessly-proliferating moral puzzles of our darkened existence ... The claim of *St. Urbain's Horseman* to enduring excellence is that it offers an alternative vision to *The Trial*, revealing despair as one extreme of the human psyche, rather than a sombre anticipation of our collective future. The difference between the two works is nothing less than philosophical, which is, in fact, the definitive difference between the

comic and the tragic modes. And our preference for the one over the other, we should have the honesty to admit, might in the final analysis be determined less by art than by attitude. *St. Urbain's Horseman* ends in healing sleep, *The Trial* ends in murder. A pessimistic reader will see Kafka as profound, Richler as shallow; an optimistic reader may take Richler as sustaining, Kafka as devitalizing. But the business of the critic is with artistry and nothing else. Richler's intent is serious, as serious as Kafka's; on the level of aspiration, then, he can hardly be faulted. As for his accomplishment, if it is less austere than Kafka's, then it is also more prolific: what we do not have in stern allegory, we have in generous abundance of character and incident. Every reader will give his allegiance to the artistry best matched to his or her own temperament, for that is the unchanging constant with which criticism must always reckon.

My allegiance, here and most places, is with Richler although my temperament is not exactly his. For one thing, Richler is far more playful than I am. Let's face it, like Jake Hersh and Barney Panofsky, he's more playful than most of who aren't outright party animals ever are. His play, as novelist and as journalist, is also strategic. So I was both surprised and disappointed to find the essay on chess in his most recent non-fiction collection, *Belling the Cat*, so weak. Weak not only in terms of the best things in that book but extremely weak by comparison to Martin Amis's 'Chess: Kasparov vs. Karpov' in *Visiting Mrs Nabokov and Other Excursions* . *Belling the Cat* opens with a piece in which Richler says he fears he belongs 'to the last generation of novelists who could supplement their incomes, earning life-sustaining cigars and cognac money, by scribbling for the mags.' That's an odd statement on a few different counts. Do he and Martin Amis belong to the same generation? I wouldn't have thought so. Does he really think that any reader who has attended to his journalism over the years thinks of it as scribbling for luxury's sake? Richler doesn't scribble, at least, he didn't until Conrad Black's Southam Inc. made him a syndicated Sunday newspaper columnist. Expensive booze and rich dried tobacco leaves might well comfort Richler but his journalism no less than his fiction has been sustained over four decades by a thirst for knowledge and taste for honesty, in the face of ignorance and deceit wherever and whenever he's confronted them. His fiction and his journalism have also been more closely linked than people who credit Tom Wolfe with inventing 'New Journalism' in the late sixties might reckon. Richler also worries publicly that he belongs to the last generation of writers who grew up reading John Dos Passos. Not so, not in my case anyway. When Richler says, as he has often said, that his aim is to be an honest witness to his times I've always understood him to be insisting that he relies upon a passion for fact in a raw state to describe the grotesqueness of the world and is willing to employ every sort of literary technique to defeat its cheats and lies as freely in a magazine or newspaper as in a novel.

Belling the Cat is a selection of twenty-seven magazine pieces that appeared between 1960 and January 1998 together with an introductory essay on his part-time career as a magazine journalist. It's generally edgier, less snobbish and more down-to-earth than Richler's newspaper column or his monthly column in *Saturday Night*. Gathered under the headings Books and Things, Going Places, Sports, Politics, a partial list of the people, things and places Richler encounters and comments upon includes Saul Bellow in his books, Woody Allen in his movies, the Bronfmans in the whisky business, Meyer Lansky in the mob, the Reichmanns in decline, Gordie Howe on the edge of retirement, Wayne Gretzky in full blossom, Pete Rose heading for his last out, Germany in the seventies, Egypt, London, Sun City in the last days of apartheid, Marrakech, Kenya, the rise and fall of Kim Campbell and the continuing legacy of Brian Mulroney. Many are reprints from Richler's long-running column 'Books and Things' for *GQ*. *GQ* provided Richler with a modest regular income and with opportunities to travel far beyond his usual haunts after his sinecure on the panel selecting books for the Book-of-the-Month Club came to an end. Lavish as his appetites for cigars and cognac might now be, I can't help thinking that journalism has been more central and necessary to Richler's life than he now claims. Remember, I've read John Dos Passos and Richler, early and often.

For my money, the best piece of writing in the *Belling the Cat* is 'Eddie Quinn' from 1960, a profile of the promoter who brought professional wrestling to the Forum and Canadian television in the fifties. It reveals just about everything any rational person could ever want to know about sport as televised spectacle and the kinds of people who make money out of it. When Richler is on his own game, he listens and waits and lets his subjects reveal themselves through unguarded bits of dialogue. The results here and in 'Gordie', 'Gretzky in Eighty-four' and 'Pete Rose' rival his superb screen writing – fully actualized scenes from the world of professional sports that remain vivid and valid long after individual players have disappeared from our TV sets. This is news that stays news as it deflates pomposity and puritanism wherever Richler finds them. He defends Saul Bellow, Mark Twain and Woody Allen against egregious revisionists. He has great fun exposing the devices and desires of various bestselling authors in 'Just Find a Million Readers and Success Will Surely Follow.' Less witty and winsome are the pieces on Canadian politics and politicians. These pages bristle with irritability and indignation as Richler chronicles the inadequacies, venalities, and over-reaching ambitions of the petty and bourgeois egomaniacs who get elected to high office in Ottawa and Quebec City. As a political commentator, Richler is less of a stylist than he is elsewhere: he's generally too full of contempt to skewer his targets with anything other than low comedy mixed with highly inflammatory ranting. And it's in this last section of *Belling the Cat* that I could hear most clearly what bothers me most about *Barney's Version* because it's here that Richler's public voice as a newspaper columnist and Barney's private voice merge and very nearly fuse.

When I say that *Barney's Version* isn't half bad, I mean that it would be much better at about 60 per cent of its current length, 250 pages rather than four hundred and something. Richler's invention is too clever by half, or to use a Kingsley Amis locution, 'not clever ENOUGH'. Barney is very human, all too human, but he isn't very substantial (unlike Jake Hersh, he has no talent of any kind except for making too much money and making too little love to the women in his life) and he's piss-poor company outside a bar. His incessant ranting and jokiness are wearisome, even if you share some of his distaste for 'covens of correctitude', because Barney is such an intellectual fraud and so emotionally feeble he can never make the distinction between questions of taste and matters of morality in himself or in others. *Barney's Version* is an easy read but it's also boring. Am I being unfair? Maybe a bit but this is the first and only Richler book I've been impatient to finish. There was no point skimming or skipping ahead because Richler is such a master of the flashback that there's always essential pieces missing until the very end and a careless reader has to go back in search of blank spots. For me, there was no going back – not until I decided to write this. And with this return to that book, there was a flash of remembered pleasure at my first glimpse of the title. It's a very good title, memorable, funny, sly because it evokes both the purple dinosaur of children's television and John Updike's novel about a divinity professor's determination to destroy a whiz kid's attempt to prove the existence of God on his computer terminal, *Roger's Version*. As far as I'm aware, nobody else has pointed out the connection to Updike: *Roger's Version* is one of Updike's better and funnier fictions and I'm fairly certain I remember Richler once citing a couple of oh-so-serious Canadian reviews of it as yet another example of humourlessness in our national character. Both Updike's novel and Richler's are about one man's attempts to short-circuit another's creative work but the connection goes deeper. Richler replaces Updike's Christian Trinity with a more secularized but primitively potent one of his own – Barney's three wives – that incarnates the traditional pattern of the major Hindu goddesses among other mythical female triads. Clara, the first Mrs Panofsky, is creative and self-destructive, the second who is designated only as the Second Mrs Panofsky is self-regarding and creatively destructive, Miriam who comes third is compassionate and nurturing. Only the Second Mrs Panofsky really comes to life: the First is a *faux* Sylvia Plath, the Third is a weakened version of Pauline in *Joshua, Then and Now*. Second Mrs Panofsky, Barney's memory losses and Richler's tweaking his nose at Margaret Atwood's *Surfacing* with a funny, macabre and masterful way of placing a corpse where it shouldn't be are reasons enough for reading *Barney's Version*, but it's not Richler at his best and no match for Updike's *Roger's Version*. The titles of both books suggest that there are very different versions of these stories from the ones told by their narrators. Richler uses footnotes by Barney's son to correct minor factual errors and to plant suspicion that Barney is not to be entirely trusted. Updike is far subtler, more enigmatic: the dividing line between the reality of Roger's life and his imaginings is so nebulous as Roger tracks his wife's affair with a graduate student at the same time as he pursues the daughter of his half-sister that a reader is challenged to be as sceptical about everyday life as a theologian as rigorous as Kierkegaard is about God, or a particle physicist is about the atom.

Ever since his return to Montreal, it's seemed unprofitable and nearly pointless to compare Richler with Waugh. For me, the standard against which I've judged Richler's work from *St Urbain's Horseman* onwards has been Joseph Heller because they both take the side of uncommon common men to make their case against the imbecilities of North American ruling elites and the sheep-like instincts and cravings of the middle classes. *Solomon Gursky Was Here* is as darkly comic, audaciously ambitious and deft a satire of the realities of corporate rule and middle-class mythology as any non-war novel has been in the wake of *Catch-22*. After its narrative complexities, linguistic dexterities and utterly delicious parodies of so much held dear by so many in our native land, maybe I was expecting too much from *Barney's Version* in wanting it to reprise Duddy Kravitz and the other denizens of Richler's earlier fictions in its own way and yet be, at least in its satirical edge, as powerful a fusillade against the prevailing myths of our national consciousness as Joseph Heller's sequel to *Catch-22*, *Closing Time*, is to those of the USA. Richler is at his niftiest and grittiest as a social critic when he's most reportorial and Barney is far too unreliable a narrator to do the job that needs doing on the world we inhabit. Barney is just a common common man, as easily forgotten as the people he himself forgets.

Grosvenor Avenue, West, Side, February 1971

Tales Catching Tales

(A Little Riding Around the Mountain
with Hood's Red Kite in My Backpack)

The enduring paradox of religion is that so much of its substance
is demonstrably false, yet it remains a driving force in all societies.
— *Sociobiology,* Edward O. Wilson

*When I decided to kill myself late in the winter of 1967, I wanted it to look
like an accident. So no suicide note or much mess. I was calm and level-
headed about it. I wasn't angry at anybody. I spent a few minutes tidying
up my room a little, just a little. No sudden departures, no quick changes. I
left books and papers scattered every which way on my desk as they always
were, as if I had every intention of returning, but I scooped up all the poems
I'd been writing about death and stuffed them into an envelope together
with a few very personal souvenirs I didn't want the authorities to find and
return to my family. I left my bank book and important personal papers in
a clearly visible place, emptied the overflowing ashtray and made my bed.
Then I showered and shaved.*

*A guy who ran the folk and blues club in downtown Ottawa where I
spent many of my Saturday nights called me 'Bond' as in James Bond, more
for my clothes than the body inside and the nickname stuck with some of
my friends. I had a closet full of fine clothes — perks from summer jobs as a
salesman in a department store. That day, I dressed in my favourite black
suit which I'd had made-to-measure — a sharply pressed very fashionable
number with a high three button front, narrow lapels, side vents, stovepipe
trousers — a grey-and-white pinstriped shirt, a black knit tie. I pulled on my
ankle-high black suede Beatle boots: I could slide a mile on ice in them. In
front of the full-length mirror on the inside of my closet door, I straightened
my trouser legs, sleeves, shoulders, collar, tie, and shot my cuffs. A bit bulky,
a touch uncool. Underneath I was wearing thick winter underwear that I
normally wore only when I went skating but there was a cold fog out and I
didn't want to be uncomfortable. Also, I figured it would weigh a ton when*

111

wet. I needed weight. I'd dropped to 128 pounds on a large-boned six-foot frame.

Tying a silk scarf loosely at my throat before pulling on my black cash-mere overcoat, snap-brim fedora and gloves, I left my room with the envelope under my arm. There was nobody in the corridors between my room and the exit. I set off on the walk I'd been taking by myself every Thursday afternoon. Along the way, I carefully disposed of my poems and souvenirs in a refuse container at the construction site for the National Arts Centre.

I was two minutes early for my appointment, three minutes later than I usually was.

'How have things been this week?'

'I did what you suggested. I tried to visualize myself in twenty years.'

'And what did you see?'

'I saw myself working in the country, half an hour outside Regina, at a place called Lumsden, Saskatchewan. I'm living there and teaching in the city, part-time at the university. History is my subject. History of ideas. England in the eighteenth century. I've published my thesis and written a book but I'm prouder of the poetry even if people don't know it's mine because of the pseudonym. Three volumes, slim like everything from Faber & Faber.'

'And what were you thinking about?'

'I had a big fire burning in the fireplace. I was watching the flames.'

'Were you by yourself?'

'No, I had a dog with me.'

'Were you depressed?'

'No, just regretful. You can't live without regrets, can you? I mean people can't unless they're really vain, can they?'

'Why do you think that's the case?'

'They don't do enough. They do too much.'

'What about you? What were you regretting?'

'Me? Missed opportunities – wife, kids, a better job, smarter books – the usual bullshit.'

'Why do you call them that?'

I backed off into silence. The therapist was a nice guy. I knew he had a pregnant wife and probably dreamed of kids, pets, a tenured position, lots of published articles to his credit, a place in the country, dogs. I knew he was sensitive, not sensitive enough to write poetry like mine but enough to feel he'd failed when he heard of my death. He'd know it wasn't altogether accidental. He was over thirty. Or seemed so. I was twenty-three.

'Tell me about the lake.'

'Which lake?'

'The one outside your country place.'

'There isn't one. The nearest lake to Lumsden is called Long Lake. It's the one my uncle drowned in, the one I told you about. That's the real resort area. Lumsden is just a small town in a valley with a river running through it. It has a ski hill.'

'Oh, like the Laurentians. Where I come from.'

'Don't think so. I've never gone skiing. I'm afraid of heights.'

'But you're more afraid of water, aren't you?'

Deathly so but that fear hadn't kept me from walking along Sussex Drive after my last few sessions with this psychologist at the university's health clinic and wandering into Rockcliffe and watching the ice crack and buckle on the Ottawa River with the slow coming of spring. I'd picked out an accessible spot on the shore from which I could glide out on the ice and keep sliding in my Beatle boots until the ice gave way beneath me and the black waters swallowed me up. I had it all worked out and it would have worked for me that Thursday except for the fog. Fog everywhere when I emerged from the clinic. Fog very thick in Major Hill park, fog shrouding monuments, fog pinching my fingers and toes, fog in my eyes and throat and seeping into my brain, fog joining earth and sky. Fog up the river, fog down the river, fog inside my head. Should I do it? Could I do it? Couldn't I? Shouldn't I? Confusion. Fog and more fog. Inside. Outside. And I still don't understand how it happened but the river's edge was closer to me than expected and open with black water. There was no chance to glide and slide slowly over sheets of ice beyond the point of no return and then there was the necessity of hurling myself downwards to meet death in a onrush of darkness and I screwed up courage to end my indecisiveness and fell forward before I was ready and stopped short held back at an odd, odd angle. Going nowhere, I began to laugh and cry and laugh.

'What did you think you were you doing down there? You could have been killed! Lucky for you I came along. That branch snagging your coat could have snapped at any time. Where did you say you lived?'

'I think it was my foot caught between the rocks that really kept me from

falling in. Saint Paul's. On Main Street.'

'*You'd better get into the cruiser. I'll drive you home. I don't think I have to file a report, do I, Father? I guess God looks out for his priests, doesn't he?'*

'*Thanks. No, I don't think anybody has to be told about this.' I didn't tell the policeman he didn't have to call me Father. I didn't tell him I was two years short of being a priest. I didn't tell him that as far as I knew, there wasn't any God looking out for me or for anybody else. If God existed, He was asleep. Me, I hadn't slept for many nights. Or days. I'd been studying God and He'd kept slipping away from me until it seemed He was nowhere to be found.*

That's the opening passage of my book *A Blue Boy in a Black Dress: A Memoir*. It was published in November 1995 and started to become a minor underground hit with readers even before it was brought to more public notice by being shortlisted for the 1996 Governor General's Award for non-fiction. While I was writing it, I knew it was going to interest some readers, judging by David Helwig's reaction, but he couldn't convince me that its readership potential extended very far. I figured him, me, Ann, some members of my extensive family, a few friends and maybe a couple of hundred general readers, most of whom I imagined would be ex-priests or ex-seminarians who had put their service in the Catholic Church behind them. I never imagined that it would have any positive appeal to practising Catholics: for many, it doesn't and I have a couple of nasty reviews clipped from pro-Papacy magazines to prove it. So I was startled to discover through a mutual friend that a very Catholic couple – Hugh Hood and his wife, the artist Noreen Mallory, liked it a lot – and they didn't even know then that much of the telling of my story and especially the passage I've quoted took shape in a room with a view into one of Hugh Hood's own stories.

When most of my book had been written and much of the winter of 1995 was over, David Helwig said to me, 'There's something you're not telling. I don't know what it is but this book will never really work until you write it.'

We were sitting in the front room of his flat on Avenue de Chateaubriand in the Plateau district of Montreal. We were sitting there, drinking tea and editing my manuscript, because David had asked me to write *A Blue Boy in a Black Dress* for a series of personal essays he's been editing for Oberon at irregular intervals over several years. The collection includes such good things as David Lewis Stein's *Going Downtown: Reflections on Urban Progress* (1993) and Peter Harcourt's *A Canadian Journey: Conversations with Time* (1994) and David Helwig's own *The Child of Someone* (1996). When David first suggested I contribute to this series, he asked for something of about 30,000 words that contrasted a personal portrait of my first twenty-five years with my second twenty-five in terms of a larger view of religion in Canada over the past half-century. This was just before Christmas 1994 and caught me off guard: it wasn't a book that I'd been planning to write just then. But I decided to go ahead with it and as soon as I had ten thousand words on paper, David and I started meeting once a week to discuss and shape what was emerging. On Friday afternoons around lunchtime usually, we'd meet at a coffee shop near where I teach and I'd hand over my latest output and he'd take it home, read it and phone me and we'd talk for half an hour or so just before he left his flat for choir practice at the Anglican Church of St John the Evangelist. But as Easter drew nearer and St John's choir started rehearsing more complex music, the editorial relationship between us deepened until I was confident enough to go to his place and talk about revisions face to face. That Friday afternoon, I looked out David's front window. Snow had fallen a couple of days earlier. It still looked fresh in this street of little traffic. There was pale sunshine, weakened by heavy clouds. David's side of the street was darkly shadowed but across the road, some brilliant rays reflected back off a window in a door a few feet higher than where I was standing. I looked up at that shining pane of glass and recognized something I hadn't been conscious of on an earlier visit I'd made to that room on Avenue de Chateaubriand. I saw that the door opposite opened into the rooms occupied by Tom and his wife in 'Light Shining Out of Darkness' in Hugh Hood's *Around the Mountain* (1968). It's one of my favourite stories in what I'd say is Hood's best book. I said to David, 'I suppose you mean my attempted suicide. I don't know if I can write about it but I'll try.'

South of Boulevard Mont-Royal as far as Rachel, from the Main eastwards past Papineau, lies the country of the ruelles. Close to the Main are streets like Henri-Julien, de Bullion, Hôtel de Ville, one way north or south, which in another place might be considered slums; not in Montréal. Going past Christoph-Colomb towards de Lanaudière, Fabre, past des Erables and Parthenais, you discover small enclaves which are clearly the homes of comfortable older citizens; the grocery stores grow imperceptibly more prosperous in appearance, their paint is fresher.

Ah, but Henri-Julien, Drôlet, that's the real thing. Hundreds of young families with three or four children, the youngest a bare-bottomed infant crawling along the ruelle curb, already trained to evade the creeping delivery vans which sometimes bump along the pitted track, while his sister, maybe four, in a smudged undershirt, eyes him as he learns his way ...

They are narrow blocks, buildings fronting on parallel main streets and backing on a shared alley.... When these streets were laid out, before the turn of the century, there was no automobile traffic, and there are no private driveways in the district. The houses, and the enormous stately multi-family dwellings, not precisely apartment buildings, crowd against each other. Back of them are the alleys which once upon a time must have béen long networks of stables. They aren't a convenient width for automobile traffic, though you can get a car in or out. Trying to ease into a former stable, you have to scramble around a very sharp right angle as you aim for the door. It's tricky in snow.

On the lesser thoroughfares, the houses will be painted brick, doorways flush with the sidewalk, three storeys high, and very often they will have ornamental cornices in wood painted light green, pale blue, most frequently pink. Atop these cornices there will be two or three little minarets or globes or vanes, all in woodwork. When you examine them closely, they are evidently not the work of master craftsmen who worked in extreme detail; there are no intricate carvings, no highly developed skill. They are the work of adze and plane, executed roughly, the same shapes repeated hundreds of times all through the neighbourhood, but never too close together. From the sidewalk there is an impression of delightful variety, heightened by the colours of successive thick coats of paint.

You enter the house directly from the sidewalk, there being

neither areaway nor front garden, nor is there space between houses. The windows have snow shutters, again executed in rough but useful carpentry. In the poorer parts of the district, the shutters are sometimes missing, the windows inadequately boarded over and the house left empty. But mostly these places present a rich family life which, having no outlet in front but the sidewalk, tends to proliferate in the back alley, safer for the abundance of babies. Sometimes back there you'll find a small, balding grass plot with ten adults roosting on it and God knows how many kids hollering ... toy trucks with a wheel gone, orange plastic Really-Ride-'Em tractors.... [Y]ou'll find a kind of dwelling that is perhaps indigenous. I mean those long rows of tall uninterrupted buildings that can't be called apartment buildings because the units are not connected by interior corridors, nor, very often, by heating lines. These huge piles are approached by outside staircases – the beautiful Montréal staircases, front and rear, so that you don't enter the building and traverse a hall to reach your front door. You climb an outside staircase and enter an independent dwelling, often separated from the rest of the building except by the plumbing. You will heat your home at your own expense with one or another of those space heaters which each winter effect multiple accidental fires and smotherings. There is something very montréalais about such buildings, which combine independence with strength and bulk. Yet the staircases are often of an extraordinary pleasing lightness and apparent fragility, front and back. Take a look at Le Montagnard which fronts on Saint-Hubert and backs on ... well, it ought to back on an alley but actually backs on Avenue de Chateaubriand, which makes me think of Atala and René, and of the gypsies in Canada.

I've quoted this opening to Hood's 'Light Shining Out of Darkness' at greater than usual length because, ah, I must confess I sometimes like copying out some of Hugh Hood's sentences almost as much as I like copying any of Mavis Gallant's at any time for the sheer pleasure of the thing. That's true as far as it goes but my larger purpose is to go further and to draw attention not just to the tonal effects of his sentences but to a fact so obvious in *Around the Mountain* that some people seem to miss it entirely: the central character in these stories is the island that's Montreal. A reader is two and a half pages into a story that doesn't quite run ten before anyone is named. Then, you're inside the Gérard Marcil Tavern, corner Saint-Hubert and Duluth, waiting for Lazarovitch with Shvetz and the narrator. They want to talk to Petroff, the patriarch of Montreal Gypsies. Lazarovitch comes and they do talk to Petroff but only briefly of beer and clarinets and dancing bears before conversation turns into a discussion of freedom and responsibility that the narrator doesn't follow. Lazarovitch phones Tom from the pay phone and they leave Petroff in the tavern. Then this:

> If you blink you'll miss Avenue de Chateaubriand. In this part of town, it really is an alley with pretensions, too narrow for cars to pass. It starts at Roy and runs north just past Marie-Anne where it is interrupted by the railroad right-of-way, the iron curtain of Montréal which severs the life flow of all the streets in the east end except the biggest, as far out as D'Iberville. North of the tracks it begins again somewhere back of de Fleurimont, running into the north end where it gradually becomes a real street.
>
> Where Tom lives you can't park. To do so, you'd have to climb right up on the sidewalk, and at that it would be hard for somebody else to get past. Sometimes at the north end of this block an undertaker parks a hearse for several hours, and then the street is effectively closed off. As in an alley, the big buildings fronting on the next main street present their backs to the passer-by. Tom lives in what must be the back part of Le Montagnard or one of its neighbours on Saint-Hubert: but for him the entrance is on de Chateaubriand. The approach to his third floor quarters is embellished by a really beautiful spiral staircase with a delicate iron railing rising in a graceful curve. I don't deny the staircase is dangerous in winter, when you can't put your bare hand on the railing, and when you have to watch your footing very carefully.
>
> As we ascended Lazarovitch said, 'A man fell down here one night straight to the bottom. He was a Hungarian, may have been drunk. Killed instantly.' It was hellishly dark climbing, but as we came to the second floor, a blind shot up on the door to your left and bright light streamed out; a pair of female eyes glared angrily

at us. Then suddenly the blind descended and it was as dark as before. On the third-floor platform, right at the top, you're apt to feel slightly dizzy if you look down at the black rectangle below, whose centre, an oblong grass plot, is ringed by upwards-pointing metal spikes. There is the impression of an elevator shaft of indefinite length, without entry except from above.

It was very dark on the balcony. All at once a door flew open and we were flooded and surrounded by intensely bright light. Tom stood in the doorway, beckoning us in. Lazarovitch went first, then Shvetz, then me. While introductions were circulating, I stood blinking and looking around, a little confused by the wave of light and colour. I had a rich, mixed impression of much pale electric light in which were splashed patch after patch of brilliant colour, high up in the room. I scarcely understood the introductions except to get the sense that I was meeting Tom and his wife, old friends of Lazarovitch.

As my eyes grew more accustomed to the light, I saw that all over the room, mounted on dully shining polished wooden stands, on top of the taller articles of furniture, stood a great fleet of what seemed at first to be children's toy sailboats.

These toy sailboats are, in fact, detailed models of famous sailing vessels of the sixteenth and seventeenth centuries, a miniaturist's works of art. Tom is a model builder for the Maritime Museum. But his life work is to replace Petroff as leader of the Gypsies in Canada. In Tom's spare time, he's preparing the first scientific lexicon of Romany. There's a discussion of philology that once again the narrator doesn't follow and then he leaves with Lazarovitch and Shvetz. When the narrator returns in the summer, Tom and his wife have moved on. So? What does it all mean? In a single paragraph between the model ships and the discussion of Tom's role in Gypsy life, the narrator observes this:

Sometimes a calm scene like this, a rounded period in the life of the imagination, will rest in one's faculties, stay, rotate, restate itself over and over in changing colours and meanings, exciting feelings, instincts, memory, imagination, seeming to have special powers to enlighten and give form to the rest of our lives.

Standing there in the queer narrow living room, almost a scarcely enclosed balcony projecting over nothing, a bit drafty, a bit poor in its other furnishings, I was mysteriously overwhelmed by this various and splendid light with feelings of a hidden and immense joy. I was smiling and transfixed, and the remembrance of the sight long after retains the capacity to direct and strengthen all my feelings, so that the life of de Chateaubriand mixes itself irrecoverably with my suspicions of the possibility of goodness, of the memorable life.

Indeed, the life of Avenue de Chateaubriand does mix itself irrecoverably with my own suspicions of the possibility of goodness, of the memorable life. The central character in this story is the island that's Montreal and what plot this story and the other stories in *Around the Mountain* do have arise less from the ways the human characters interact with one another than with the ways *l'esprit montréalais* becomes a *présence d'esprit*, a presence of mind in the human beings dwelling beneath that sign of the cross on the heights of Mount Royal. For the narrator and for all his readers. Hood is a model of universalism among fellow Catholics, a firm believer in the influence of the Holy Spirit and the gifts It is said to bring –- wisdom, counsel, understanding – I hope you know the rest.

In his 'Author's Introduction' to *The Collected Stories: IV, Around the Mountain*, Hood writes

> The book was intended as a documentary/fantasy portrait of the city and its people, politics, folkways, geography, and appearance. It was meant to appeal to tourists visiting the city during Expo summer, and to residents of Montréal who might wish to acquire a souvenir of those heady months more lasting than a T-shirt or stuffed animal bearing the embroidered legend 'Man and His World'. I wrote the book from mixed motives, one of them purely opportunistic. I believed naively that I might achieve a popular success.

Whatever his original intention, Hugh Hood created something not just new in Canadian writing but a literary concept I think might just be original in English language literature with this book of twelve stories that link one Christmas to another, roughly month by month, and form a circle around the peak of the low hill that English Montrealers call 'the mountain.' To my way of thinking, this book is so utterly original that even Hood (who sometimes sees more deeply with greater critical acumen into his own work than most authors ever do) sees *Around the Mountain* in a more modest and fragmented way than it ought to be viewed. The 'Author's Introduction' was composed twenty-six years after completion of the book and Hood's reflections on his original motives recognize 'that other projects were also inscribed in the conception' – projects such as pleasing readers who like to trace patterns of verbal cross-references through close reading and secondly, representing his religious experience as a Catholic 'by birth, upbringing, and mature conviction' through a series of references to Dante's *Purgatorio* and Wordsworth's *Prelude:*

> Can there be such a thing as a 'secular religious narrative poem'? That's more or less what I hoped *Around the Mountain* might turn out to be, a work that would carry on its face an innocent air of immersion in this world, the fallen secular community, so that at the crucial half-way point in the series of linked stories I could pause and transfer to humanity itself two of the attributes of the Divine presence. 'Human purpose,' I dared to write, 'is inscrutable but undeniable'.
>
> I wanted those acute (women) readers to take note of this transferral of the Divine to the human, and to understand that the mis/attribution was meant as part of the allusion game, that inscrutability and undeniability remain properly speaking attributes of absolute presence alone. I was then and have remained an essentialist aesthete, God help me, just the worst sort of person to be in these times.

Can there be such a thing as a secular religious narrative poem? That's something I'll leave to others to answer. If there is, this book ain't it! I did say that Hood *sometimes* sees to the depths of his work with great acumen: at other times, he *stretches* things quite a bit with more impish analogies than his critics seem to notice. What we have here is much closer to a novel than a narrative poem, an extended fiction that's a little like Malcolm Lowry's *Under the Volcano* in its use of a volcanic mountain (albeit a worn-to-extinction one) as the central character and a little in the tradition of John Cowper Powys's *A Glastonbury Romance* in its emphasis on the inscrutable yet undeniable presence of God. More obscurely, some of the 'fantasy' in his portraits veers close to what the great and greatly neglected T.F. Powys, John Cowper's brother, does in the name of religious fable. That said, Hugh Hood stakes out a territory none of these earlier authors envisioned, because while studying at Saint Michael's College in Toronto with Marshall McLuhan in the early fifties, he learned more about living in the presence of death, about the God in Jesus who triumphs over death, and about adopting an un-self-conscious naiveté in the service of that God than were available to those earlier writers.

Hugh Hood describes himself as an essentialist aesthete. And what's one of those when it's at home? I think you probably have to be at least a little older than I am, have read at least as many books by Jacques Maritain as I have and retained their contents better than I ever did, have studied Hood's dissertation that discussed the theory of imagination in the Romantic poets and earned him a doctorate in English literature from the University of Toronto in 1955 and, most important of all, retain at the very least a Lutheran or High Anglican belief (if Catholicism is beyond your ken) in the Real Presence of Christ in the Eucharist to grasp essentialist aestheticism in at least as many of its nuances as might appear in any one of Hood's seven collections of stories, fifteen or so novels, three essay collections and other assorted works. Here's Hood's own bash at its broad outline:

> What we are united to in this world is not the physical insides of persons or things, but the knowable principle in them. Inside everything that exists is essence, not in physical space and time, but as forming space and time and the perceptions possible within them. What I know, love and desire in another person isn't inside him like a nut in a shell, but is everywhere that he is, forming him. My identity isn't inside me — it is how I am. It's hard to express the way we know the form of things, but this is the kind of knowing that art allows us.

Art after all, like every other human activity, implies a philosophical stance; either you think there is nothing to things that is
not delivered in their appearance, or you think that immaterial
forms exist in these things, conferring identity on them. These
are not the only ontological alternatives but they are extreme
ones, and they state a classical ontological opposition. The bias of
most contemporary thought has been toward the first alternative,
until the very recent past. But perhaps we are again beginning to
be able to think about the noumenal element in things, their
essential and intelligible principles, what Newman called the 'illative' aspect of being. The danger in this is that you may dissolve
the hard, substantial shapes of things, as they can be seen to be,
into an idealistic mish-mash – which is something I'm not
inclined to do. I'm not a Platonist or a dualist of any kind. I think
with Aristotle that the body and the soul are one; the form of a
thing is totally united to its matter. The soul is the body. No idea
but in things.

That is where I come out; the spirit is totally *in* the flesh. If you
pay close enough attention to things, stare at them, concentrate
on them as hard as you can, not just with your intelligence, but
with your feelings and instincts, you will begin to apprehend the
forms in them. Knowing is not a matter of sitting in an armchair
while engaged in some abstruse conceptual calculus of weights
and measures and geometrical spaces. Knowing includes making
love, and making pieces of art, and wanting and worshipping *and*
calculating (because calculation is also part of knowing) and in
fact knowing is what Wordsworth called it, a 'spousal union' of
the knower and the known, a marriage full of flesh.... Things are
full of visionary gleam.

That's taken from 'The Ontology of Super-Realism' in his 1973 essay collection *The Governor's Bridge Is Closed*. The piece was written originally
for the anthology *The Narrative Voice* (1972) as an explanatory introduction to the stories 'Socks' and 'Boots'. Just the thing for college students
nearly three decades ago! Now!
 'Philosophy is a great subject for proclaiming beginnings, for
drawing lines in the conceptual sand, for declaring wholly new ways of

thinking about very old questions,' the wonderfully clear-headed and cogent Mark Kingwell wrote recently in a review of the Phoenix edition of *The Great Philosophers* in the *Globe and Mail*. 'It is equally, the discipline whose eternal subject is its own demise. Nothing is more common than for a philosopher to declare all previous philosophizing outmoded, irrelevant, useless or (worst of all) merely nonsensical.' Which is one reason for my avoiding it here. Another is that I was only ever good enough at it to earn a slightly above average undergraduate degree in it at the hands of a half-dozen Basilian priest teachers, most of whom held postgraduate degrees from St Michael's College that they'd earned about the same time Hugh Hood was there. One of the reasons that I was never any better at doing what they were attempting to teach me to do in the name of philosophy is that it seems I've always been more interested in what people say about things than in how the truth of the matter stands. To me, arguments are more or less interesting and Hood's lines in the conceptual sand are interesting because they articulate an aesthetic that's both very dark and potentially very comic. The architects of Bauhaus were fond of saying 'form follows function,' a conceptual framework that's as easy to take in as any modern building. What Hood is saying isn't a reversed 'function follows form' – 'fish have fins and they swim', the way I learned to read Aristotle – but 'function is form'. This is very dark because it makes essential knowledge a matter of imagination and intuition that is guaranteed certainty only when fully revealed by God and inscrutable He isn't saying or showing much. In His absence, essential knowledge comes through artists, the most unreliable of creatures on God's earth. The comedy comes from the fact that most of us labour with very limited imaginations and screwball intuitions most of the time. That's what accounts for Hood's great love for James Thurber, P.G. Wodehouse and Evelyn Waugh.

* * *

There are moments, quite frequent these days, when I'd like to talk with Hugh Hood about the darkness of his aesthetic credo and explore its roots with him. I don't mean – God forbid – psychological roots. What I do mean is the ways in which his interpretation of essentialism is less dependent on Aristotle than on the philosophical traditions of the University of Paris that arose in defence of Catholicism against Martin

Luther's attack on Aristotle. There's much to be said on that point (but not here and not now) and on such things growing out of it as Guy Debord's *Society of the Spectacle*, Marshall McLuhan's *The Gutenberg Galaxy* and Hood's own works. The closest Hood has come to detailing any of it is his essay 'The Intuition of Being: Morley, Marshall & Me' in his 1991 collection *Unsupported Assertions* where he writes of Jacques Maritain's influence on Callaghan, McLuhan and himself:

> We cannot name God as God is, but we can intuit that all that exists is analogous to the Divine Existence, in due proportion to the nature of individual things. The whole of Being is a multiform system of analogical relations in which everything that is pos-sesses a mode of being, and to that degree bears a proportionate analogical relationship to the Almighty.... The specific and unmistakable McLuhan wit and humour are largely based on analogies of proportion.

And Hood's own. It's something worth discussing.

My desire to talk with him is full of regret: Hugh Hood died on August 1, 2000 – the same day that the proofs of this essay were pulled from the press. His death came as a shock even though I knew he was in poor health. For the last many, many months of his life, he was held fast to his home by a degenerative disease that made conversation difficult and wearying. What energy he had he spent completing works in progress and maintaining connections within his family. I'd met Hugh more than once and I believe I might have had him for a friend, but I preferred to keep a distance, because I admired him so much, and I wanted to be able to write about his books without feeling influenced or constrained by a personal relationship. Book reviews are written for the sake of readers not writers: not all writers see it this way. For me, the absence of a possible friendship is preferable to the compromising of a review or personal disloyalty. My rule of thumb is to keep my distance from writers I don't already know whose books I really want to review. Hugh Hood is a writer who I wanted to write about as soon as I dis-covered him. That was just about the time I settled in Montreal in 1973, the year of *The Governor's Bridge Is Closed*. That's when Hugh Hood was just about as well known and respected as Mordecai Richler – at least in

Montreal. So what I know of Hood comes from his three books of essays, his introductions to the collected stories, from talking to people we both know well, and from the fascinating telephone conversations I had with him every time I reviewed one of his longer fictions.

Hugh Hood began writing short fiction in January 1957 in West Hartford, Connecticut, where he was teaching at Saint Joseph College. This was a year and a bit after graduating from the University of Toronto. He says that he had no theory of his own writing, belonged to no school and had no formed sense of himself as a Canadian writer. He began writing in the hope that with much practice and painstaking labour he might be able to write for *Esquire*, *The New Yorker* and the literary quarterlies. Between January 1957 and March 1962 when he started to assemble his first published book, *Flying a Red Kite*, he wrote thirty-eight stories as well as two complete unpublished novels. And made it into the August 1960 issue of *Esquire* with 'After the Sirens', a story about the aftereffects of a nuclear explosion that has been widely reprinted and is known by a lot of people around the world who know nothing else by Hugh Hood. He was tentatively offered the position of assistant to Rust Hills, the fiction editor at *Esquire*, a job he turned down in favour of an appointment to the Faculté des Lettres de Université de Montreal. It can't have been an easy decision – money and fame in America or teaching English literature at a French university in Montreal? A position in Outremont had many more attractions to offer the bilingual Professor Hood in 1961 than a job in Westmount offered unilingual me in 1973, and I found it irresistible. Then again, my choice was between college teaching in Montreal and advertising agency copywriting in Toronto: what I wanted most was to live in a place I knew it was possible to write about – the city of Leonard Cohen and Mordecai Richler, Gabrielle Roy and Hugh Hood. Something similar may have swayed Hood – when he came, Montreal was the city of Hugh MacLennan, and MacLennan was living proof that it was possible to be a more than competent scholar, a fine university teacher, a serious fiction writer and a popular novelist who was dealing with the question of national unity in a bicultural society and that it would be possible to be all these things at the same time. MacLennan was also a moral realist and that too is what Hood wanted to be – 'not a naturalist nor a surrealist nor a magic realist nor in any way an experimental or *avant-garde* writer,' he writes in 'The Ontology of Super-Realism'. The passage continues:

> All my early writing dealt with the affairs of credible characters in more or less credible situations. As I look back, I see that this instinctive moral realism was tempered by an inclination to show these credible characters, in perfectly ordinary situations, doing violent and unpredictable, and even melodramatic, things. A brother and sister go to visit their mother's grave and are unable to find it in a cemetery of nightmarish proportions; a man kills his newly baptized girl friend thinking that she will go straight to Heaven; a young priest molests a child sexually; a young boy goes mad under great strain. A yachtsman runs his boat on a rock and sinks it, drowning his wife and her lover, who are trapped below deck. I would never choose actions like these nowadays because of their improbability. I still write about intense feeling that leads to impulsive and sometimes violent acts, but I'm better able to locate these feelings in credible occasions.
>
> In those days, and for several years afterwards, I tried to control these melodramatic tendencies – murder, suicide, hanging about in cemeteries, drowning – by a strong sense of the physical form of stories. I arranged my pieces according to complex numerologies ... *Around the Mountain* follows the calender very precisely, with one story for each month from one Christmas to the next. I've always had a fondness for the cycle of the Christian liturgical year.

In March of 1962, Hugh Hood committed himself to bring out a first collection of stories with Ryerson Press in Toronto. *Flying a Red Kite* was edited for that press by Robert Weaver and John Robert Colombo who were then co-editing the *Tamarack Review*. Hood's first book covers a lot of ground with a great wash of accomplishment and gusts of brilliance. He's trying his hand at stories of several different kinds that are aimed at different readerships. There are stories under the influence of New York and *The New Yorker*, a range that extends from the topicality and mass appeal of a tale of nuclear disaster in 'After the Sirens' to a memoir about a summer job in Toronto, 'Recollections of the Works Department' (that stands up very well after a half-dozen readings). There's a pair of big literary stories aimed at the old *Kenyon Review*'s academic readership. But it also includes the title story and others that announce a new, unusually gifted and essentially Montreal storyteller with a sense of style previously unknown in this country's writers and a voice all his own.

A couple of the stories in *Flying a Red Kite* first appeared in the *Tamarack Review* and Robert Weaver and John Robert Colombo advanced Hood's career further by making him their man at Expo 67. In the five years between the publication of his first book and the coming of the World's Fair to Montreal, Hood published his first novel *White Figure, White Ground* (1964) and prepared his second novel, *The Camera Always Lies*, and his second story collection, *Around the Mountain*, for publication in Canada's Centennial year. By 1967 he was also writing for popular magazines and doing radio broadcasts: Peter Gzowski had him writing about NHL expansion teams for the *Star Weekly* and both the CBC and NFB were producing his stories. It was around this time that Robert Fulford, then of the *Toronto Star*, advised Hood in print to stop wasting his time writing novels 'devoid of psychological penetration' when he had such finely honed skills for recording the outsides of things so accurately. That's advice I felt like echoing when I read the first two novels and then the third and fourth – *A Game of Touch* (1970) and *You Can't Get There from Here* (1972). It wasn't the absence of psychological penetration that bothered me then and bothers me now in his longer fictions. Or compelling plots. Hood is at his best when he's anecdotal and I find nothing wrong in novels built upon anecdote – Joyce's *Ulysses*, Woolf's *To the Lighthouse*. The danger with essentialist aestheticism, as Hood noted, is that it readily dissolves 'the hard, substantial shape of things, as they can be seen to be, into an idealistic mishmash.' It's not something he was inclined to do within the compass of the short stories he was writing then or later, especially not when a Montreal locale crowds his vision. In aiming for wider targets and deeper fields, the early novels turn quixotic – literally so as Hood tilts at the worlds of painting, film and cartooning in the first three and at the corporate forces at work within a developing African nation in the fourth. I simply can't read any of them with quiet enjoyment: I keep finding myself turning into Sancho Panza, that great Erasmus-inspired proponent of a better-ordered world in which wisdom is scepticism combined with empirical judgement.

In his introduction to *Flying a Red Kite* in *The Collected Stories: Vol. I*, Hood writes:

> The resources of a writer of fiction are deeply divided, but fortunately into only two parts. He or she can derive story material either from observation of the external world and from material communicated by other such observers, in short from experience, from what has actually happened to him and others, or he can derive material from the inner world of imagination and reflection. These are the two wells at which one drinks. Any writer's stories therefore can be shown to be stories of observation or imagination, or a composite of the two. Naturally most fiction is of the third kind. I have often been treated as a writer who relies upon actuality, on what has happened, for his material, whereas I know myself to be a writer in whose work imagination and fantasy, the purely private and extra-historical take the primary place.

Well, as someone famously remarked, there are people who divide the world into two kinds of people and those who don't. Having denied that he's a Platonist or dualist of any kind, Hood shows himself here to be doing a bit of a dance to Kant's bifurcating jig, and Maritain's, come to that. The trouble with artists who live by ideas is that all too often their art dies at the hands of an idea: Hood's imagination and fantasy are far less pure in their privacy and extra-historicity and far more shaped by mass media than he ever seems to credit. The proof is in the perplexity that anyone fifteen or more years younger than Hood and less rooted in radio days, pre-war Hollywood movies and the ethos of Southern Ontario feels in the presence of these early novels: the details are never quite in focus in terms of experience, nor are they as severely distorted as reflections are thought to be. Getting things wrong in uninteresting ways is a foible Hood has in common with Michael Ondaatje and Robertson Davies. Happily in Hood's case, he's brighter than that dim old bulb of Davies and less opaque in delivery than Ondaatje. What makes even the lesser of his better works more readable than any of theirs is his 'natural talent' to describe, evoke, and conjure the surrounding atmosphere of the *illative* – the thinginess of things – clearly in a relaxed conversational idiom and tone. Here's the conclusion of 'Flying a Red Kite'. Anyone interested in finer points of language ought to note the ready switch from highly syntactic to highly paratactic sentence forms:

This time he gave the kite plenty of string before he began to move; he ran as hard as he could, panting and handing the string out over his shoulders, burning his fingers as it slid through them. All at once he felt the line pull and pulse as if there were a living thing on the other end and he turned on his heel and watched while the kite danced into the upper air-currents above the treetops and began to soar up and up. He gave it more line and in an instant it pulled high up away from him across the fence, two hundred feet and more above him over the cemetery where it steadied and hung, bright red in the sunshine. He thought flashingly of the priest saying 'it's all a sham', and he knew all at once that the priest was wrong. Deedee came running down to him, laughing with excitement and pleasure and singing joyfully about the gingerbread man, and he knelt in the dusty roadway and put his arms around her, placing her hands on the line between his. They gazed, squinting in the sun, at the flying red thing, and he turned away and saw in the shadow of her cheek and on her lips and chin the dark rich red of the pulp and juice of the crushed raspberries.

I've lost track of the number of time I've read 'Flying a Red Kite'. There came a time in the eighties, not long after the publication of my first novel, *The Education of J.J. Pass*, when the *tristesse* of my last days in the seminary returned and engulfed me: I was sad, lonely, melancholic, chronically depressed. Not unto serious thoughts of death. People are said to die of broken hearts: Does anyone die because a first novel that has been enthusiastically reviewed isn't a runaway success with the reading public and its author is struck by the sophomore jinx? Unlike Hugh Hood, I'd never thought of myself as a writer of short stories. Unlike a lot of writers and would-be writers, I'd never made any serious attempt to write a short story until I'd completed three novels and a couple of novellas. A batch of stories started forming in my mind and flowing from my fingers as I revised the third of the novels and a half-dozen of them were published effortlessly in small magazines. The stories seemed like a small and happy bonus. Oberon published a novella from among them, 'Hans Denck, Cobbler', together with one by Mike Mason as a *A Beast with Two Backs* while awaiting delivery of my novel *The Education of J.J. Pass*. I thought that I could follow up the publication of this first novel, the third I'd written, with a novel already completed that I thought very nearly as good – a still unpublished *Boileau and the Buddha* – and then complete a third and a fourth in what I wanted to be an interlinked quartet. If I managed to squeeze a short story collection in there somewhere, so much the better. But Oberon didn't want *Boileau and the Buddha* and no one else did either: I broke off work on the quartet and tried a different kind of novel and nobody wanted it either. I had absolutely no difficulty finding work as a reviewer of other people's fictions but the only person who seemed to want to see fiction from me was Geoff Hancock at *Canadian Fiction Magazine*. I listened to a lot of Tom Waits songs. I went for a lot of long walks. I bought myself a bicycle. I thought long and hard about short fiction – mostly Hood's and my own.

On foot and on bike, I came to know parts of the city I hadn't previously known except in the words of other people. One of my favourite rides was whizzing through the railway underpass in Westmount and bumping over the level crossings in St Henri down through its abandoned factory sites to the bicycle path along the Lachine Canal and across the Expo bridge to St Helen's Island, the former site of Expo. I'd pack a lunch and take a book – sometimes Hood's *Flying a Red Kite*, more often *Around the Mountain* or, less frequently than either, one of his later collections, *The Fruit Man, the Meat Man and the Manager* (1971), *Dark Glasses* (1976), *None Genuine Without This Signature* (1981) or maybe the then just-published *August Nights* (1985) – and spend the middle hours of the day reading stories, watching the play of light on the river and trying to think about the craft of writing stories instead of becoming melodramatic about my own life. If it was a really bad day with a litter of black demon puppies gnawing at my innards, I'd cycle over to the Grand Prix raceway on that island. It's called the Circuit Gilles Villeneuve nowadays and I suspect they've limited access to it, but in the mid-eighties I could go from the bicycle path through a parking lot and be right on it and sprint through its twists and turns at maybe a tenth of the speed of a Formula I race car. Even at that less than Tour de France speed the demon dogs got left behind, and when I was free of them I could think more reasonably about my writing. As I cooled down with slower and slower laps around that track, it seemed more and more reasonable to me to put aside all thoughts of writing any more novels until I had created a book of short fiction that had a certain integrity of its own. Half as homage, half as a carefully deliberated repudiation of the order and essentialist aesthetic of *Around the Mountain*, I constructed *Je t'aime Cowboy:* nine stories – not twelve – in my book and a radically different geographical trajectory. Human nature was nature enough for me to document the things I found lacking in men in Montreal in the eighties.

As Hood once explained to J.R. (Tim) Struthers in an interview, *Around the Mountain* begins with the characters

> on the flat land up in the northeast of the Montreal region and they gradually make their way up to the top. In the June story they're at the top looking down from above, and that is, if you like, the holiest story.... Then it winds around the mountain and back down to the flat land north of Montreal but this time in the west. A complete rotation around the mountain from east to west takes place, and the stories are calculated to how high up the mountain they are.

This spatial structure coheres with a temporal cycle that runs through a full year from mid-December to mid-December. The June story is, as Hood says, the holiest. It's been given a good close reading by Robert Lecker in *On the Line* (1982), the kind of reading I'd like to see Lecker give the whole book one day. Until then, Keith Garebian's chapter on the short stories in *Hugh Hood* (1983) in the Twayne series says succinctly albeit prissily some of what deserves to be written out at greater length:

> [Hood] attempts to write a pastoral about Montreal which mediates between Stephen Leacock's nostalgia and Bertolt Brecht's infernal inversions. His city contains elements of both corruption and innocence, but is never purely hellish or paradisal. 'A Green

Child', where the narrator talks about the symbolic landscape of Antonioni's films of alienation, gives us the edge of the city, whose huge, unfinished building constructions look colossally impersonal and apocalyptic. The narrator descends into a valley of shadows (rue Valdombre) in quest of his fleeing green child, a girl with a green scarf, and here the colour green and vanishing illumination are emblems of the grail light…. Such contrasts attest to Hood's balancing act, which shows us multiple ways of looking at the same subject. And what is particularly subtle about this mode of vision is that it is not ironic or dualistic, but revelatory and monistic. It is all one city.

Indeed it is all one city, and what has drawn me to *Around the Mountain* time and again is less the nostalgia (which I'm not inclined to connect with Stephen Leacock) or even the Brechtian inversions (which I've attempted to rope and brand into my own literary devices and desires) but the capaciousness of Hood's Montreal. It has more characters from both sides of the language divide than is common in much writing of the time, includes local French expressions and, wonder of wonders, represents *les autres* – Montreal's Jewish artists, Gypsy craftsmen, Russian sailors and so many more. I find those like myself and those I know here in its pages. I also find the city that was here in 1967 under the city that's here now: the great additional pleasure for readers of *Around the Mountain* who live in Montreal is to go where the stories lead and see what still holds and what has been folded back, what is here and what is gone forever in cityscape and inscape.

Leonard Cohen at Morton Rosengarten's Vernissage, 1966

The Fiction of Leonard Cohen

That's everyone's dilemma: at the times we think we're coolest,
what everyone else sees is a guy with his mouth full of banana....

I'm just a famous nobody.
                    – Leonard Cohen

Whenever Leonard Cohen is mentioned, I think 'fabulous novelist,
ferociously funny, too soon finished.' I always think this but say it less
and less because I feel helplessly skewed, hopelessly eccentric in my
response: few people seem to know what I'm talking about, fewer seem
to care. Is it simply my neighbourhood? I think maybe yes, maybe no. I
live within five city blocks of the Westmount street where Leonard
Cohen grew up, a six-buck cab ride from the house on the Plateau he has
owned in Montreal through the better years of his career. Is it different
where you are?

As a novelist, Leonard Cohen is better known as a poet. As a poet,
he's better known as a song writer. As a song writer, he's better known as
a performer. As a performer, he's best known for a public persona which
isn't usually construed as comic. As the personification of world-weary,
urbane, chic suffering, he's a pop icon, so instantly recognizable that the
book designers at Random House have used a black and white image of
his face in left profile, eyes closed, on a black background as the front
and back covers on Ira B. Nadel's recent biography, *Various Positions*.
Cohen's face is encased in a clear plastic dust jacket upon which titles
have been printed in Buddhist saffron. Remove the dust jacket and
Cohen meets the reader unadorned, sideways on but only left-sided. At
first sight, I thought, ah, an error – no right profile. Then I thought, no,
Random House is cutting costs by using one photographic plate twice.
Then the joke hit me, Cohen is insisting we see less than the full picture.
In his lifelong game of outsmarting everyone who wants to appropriate
him for themselves, he's won again. With Ira B. Nadel, it wasn't much of
a contest. As a biographer, Nadel makes the fundamental mistake of

allowing Cohen to disarm him completely and beguile him into show-ing Cohen precisely as Cohen wishes to be seen — two-dimensionally and disappearing within himself.

Jacket copy identifies Nadel as the author of studies in biography and James Joyce. It says he teaches at the University of British Columbia where he's a professor of English. This suggests that *Various Positions* is a scholarly and critical work. It isn't. Professor Nadel is scholarly only in the earnestness and humourlessness of his prose: as a critic, he's just another fan offering homage. Instead of developing critical distance, he shuffles his way through a pack of index cards and selects careful comments from Cohen's friends that add more layers to the enigma wrapped within a mystery that the singer has become. Cohen can 'contain and survive elements of pain in the dark. He [i]s in touch with matters of the soul and heart,' says his old and dear friend Nancy Bacal, pointing to the light he casts in the dark. The end product is a shrunk-to-fit-the-celebrity biography that suits a novelist as inventive and comic and *outré* as Leonard Cohen as badly as a tweed jacket and polka-dot bow tie. Like any other straight-off-the-peg-to-the-pen-of-a-hack biography, *Various Positions* offers a warning to the *hoi polloi* of the extraordinary high prices even a quite ordinary superstar has to pay for fame and success. And then it glories in the triumph of its subject's will to surmount a life in pop culture, despite the costs, and to become hap-pily abnormal. Which is fine as far as it goes, I suppose, for those who need to find a threadbare moral in every *prêt-à-porter* story but it doesn't get near the naked skin of this hard-core troubadour. Even though his songs, as Ann Diamond says, 'became a weathervane of neo-conservatism about fifteen years ago' and his image has become his most important fiction, Cohen remains a subversive and dangerous novelist. But Nadel plays it safe, expends less than 5 per cent of his book on the novels and considers them as autobiographical facts, not art.

Leonard Cohen reinvented himself as a singer-songwriter at the age of thirty-two because he couldn't make a living as a poet and novelist in Canada without either (a) turning into a hip Adrienne Clarkson impersonator at the CBC or (b) finding himself a niche somewhere in the academic hierarchy and becoming an *Ur*-Ondaatje. Instead, he borrowed money and headed off to Nashville with his guitar. He got as far as New York's Chelsea Hotel. In retrospect, the make-over of

Leonard Cohen the writer into Leonard Cohen the singer seems inevitable. At the time, it was anything but a sure bet. He had a singing voice even Bob Dylan fans disliked, he was an indifferent guitar player with a five-chord repertoire, he was a decade older than anyone else who was hip and too bourgeois to be beatnik, he'd never played with professional musicians and was so heavily into tranquillizers that he'd picked up the nickname Captain Mandrax. In 1969, *Songs of Leonard Cohen* sounded so wasted and wounded, so used-up, nobody I knew could listen to the album straight through. Those of us who cared enough about Cohen's writing to worry about the writer figured he'd never make it back from the wired high where he was mainlining melancholia. That's when I started thinking of Leonard Cohen as 'fabulous novelist, ferociously funny, too soon finished'.

In 1969, I knew both novels – *The Favourite Game* and *Beautiful Losers* – and all his poetry. In this regard, I was uncommonly well-read even among Cohen fanatics. *The Favourite Game* was published in England in October 1963 and in New York in September 1964. It was available in Canada only as an import until McClelland & Stewart published a paperback off-print of the British edition in 1970. In 1968, it was a rarity loaned to me by a friend on condition that I read it in the McMaster graduate students' lounge in one sitting while he perched on the next sofa and could keep an eye on it. David was that kind of friend and *The Favourite Game* is that kind of book: if you're young and you love it, you can't let it out of your sight. Mind you, neither of us was aware what a rarity I held in my hands that day. If Nadel has done his sums right, somewhere around a thousand copies were sold in the UK and the USA combined. Nowadays, *The Favourite Game* is as common as muck and about as attractively packaged as a bag of potting soil in a $6.95 New Canadian Library reprint that features three severely mismatched type fonts and a tiny reproduction of a large Graham Coughtry oil painting in six shades of shit on the cover, together with an afterword by Paul Quarrington. What point is being made here? Paul Quarrington is the first comic writer I'd recommend as a guide for a weekend of fishing on a northern lake for anyone who drinks beer and smokes cigars and talks hockey while listening to old Beach Boy records. Is the New Canadian Library trying to attract first year engineering students to Cohen? Quarrington trolls for new Canadian readers with a foreign lure '*The*

Favourite Game ... like *David Copperfield,* falls into a subset of the *bildungsroman,* the *künstlerroman,* a novel which portrays the maturation of an artist (in German, *ein Künstler*).'

If you can swallow *bildungsroman* and the egregious comparison to Dickens without upchucking on the sick stink of word-intoxicated pseudo-Euro abstraction, you ought not to read *The Favourite Game.* It isn't *David Copperfield,* nor is it Joyce's *Portrait of the Artist as a Young Man,* let alone Mann's *Doktor Faustus.* When I first read it, it simply devoured my own words. *The Favourite Game* is a young man's book full of precisely articulated un-Teutonic follies that are so outrageously naive, so blissfully unsophisticated, so innocently unthinking that this novel just doesn't square with any hole a Northrop Frye-gean pigeon like Quarrington wants to nest it in. 'To be a writer is to use all the brains you've got' says Stephen Vizinczey in *Truth and Lies in Literature* and you don't have to look any further than Cohen's friendship with Vizinczey during the years in which *The Favourite Game* took shape to grasp its own peculiar braininess, its revel in the ability of a young man to live entirely in a middle world between sensory and intellectual realities, in the non-literal, non-rational realm of poetic imaginings. This is what makes *The Favourite Game* as poignant, hilarious and erotically-charged as Vizinczey's own *In Praise of Older Women.* Both novels were too brave and unbridled for Jack McClelland – Vizinczey published his own book and sold it door-to-door, Cohen sought publication in London and New York. And one good thing you can say about Nadel's biography is that it does provide a very clear picture of Cohen's dealings with Jack McClelland.

In April 1959, when he was twenty-four, Leonard Cohen was awarded a Canada Council grant of $2000. He used the money to live cheaply in London and even more cheaply on Hydra while drafting the novel he called *Beauty at Close Quarters.* He returned to Canada in November 1960 and secured another Canada Council grant and a rejection slip from McClelland & Stewart. Jack McClelland objected to Cohen writing prose in the first place, found his novel tedious, egotistical, disgusting and morbid in its sex, worried about its autobiographical content and suggested radical revisions without guaranteeing publication. Cohen signed contracts with Secker & Warburg for Commonwealth rights and with Viking for the States. Both publishers wanted a shorter book:

Cohen began to revise with some ambivalence. He knew he'd created something important, 'a book without alibis; not the alibis of the open road or narcotics or engaging crime.' He'd 'wanted to tell about a certain society and a certain man and reveal insights into the bastard Art of Poetry. I think I know what I'm talking about. Autobiography? Lawrence Breavman isn't me but we did a lot of the same things. But we reacted differently to them and so we became different men.' Cohen cut the book in half. It wasn't self-mutilation. He wrote Irving Layton, 'anyone with an ear will know I've torn apart orchestras to arrive at my straight, melodic line ... I walk lighter and carry a big scalpel ... I don't know anything about people – that's why I have this terrible and irresistible temptation to be a novelist.'

We're lucky he didn't resist the temptation. It seems to me astonishingly negligent that the uncut *Beauty at Close Quarters* has never been published and the two published novels are available in Canada only in the shoddy New Canadian Library edition. If M&S celebrated our literature rather than flogged it to death, they'd do as Random House does with Michael Ondaatje and offer us Cohen cut and uncut in quality trade paperbacks in a uniform edition with *Beautiful Losers* – all to Cohen's own designs. (Cohen has always had wonderful ideas about how his books should look. Nowadays, he's an accomplished computer artist.) *The Favourite Game* is not only highly readable, it remains very saleable. And not only in Montreal even though it does have special attractions for readers who co-habit its terrain:

He began his tour through the heart streets of Montreal. The streets were changing. The Victorian gingerbread was going down everywhere, and on every second corner was the half-covered skeleton of a new, flat office building. The city seemed fierce to go modern, as though it had suddenly been converted to some new theory of hygiene and had learned with horror that it was impossible to scrape the dirt out of gargoyle crevices and carved grape vines, and therefore was determined to cauterize the whole landscape....

He turned and looked at the city below him.

The heart of the city wasn't down there among the new buildings and widened streets. It was right over there at the Allan, which, with drugs and electricity, was keeping the businessmen sane and their wives from suicide and their children free from hatred. The hospital was the true heart, pumping stability and erections and orgasms and sleep into all the withering commercial limbs. His mother was sleeping in one of the towers. With windows that didn't quite open.

That's near the end. This is from the opening pages:

The Breavmans founded and presided over most of the institutions which make the Montreal Jewish community one of the most powerful in the world today.

The joke around the city is: The Jews are the conscience of the world and the Breavmans are the conscience of the Jew. 'And I am the conscience of the Breavmans,' adds Lawrence Breavman....

The feeling today, if anyone troubles himself to articulate it, is that the Breavmans are in a decline. 'Be careful,' Lawrence Breavman warns his executive cousins, 'or your children will speak with accents.'

Front to back, *The Favourite Game* is dead certain about its society and a certain Lawrence Breavman who relates his history as a poet within it. It's Jewish to the core, so steeped in biblical consciousness that Cohen has no need to draw direct analogies between his brave and bereaved protagonist and the psalmists. Breavman is simultaneously a priest exiled in Babylon mourning the loss of King Solomon's glories and King David revelling carnally in the delights of a multitude of women that includes a particularly beguiling foreigner. The book opens with the line, 'Breavman knows a girl named Shell whose ears were pierced so she could wear the long filigree earrings.' Like Suzanne in the later song, Shell has touched his body with her mind but she wants to stake a greater claim to more than his republic of flesh. Shell is a daughter of a Daughter of the American Revolution and Breavman is creating a song of songs to her glory *and* a lament over his inability to renounce his Jewish soul to her Gentile body. Breavman may be sombre but the book isn't. It's too full of delightful incongruities, weirdly twisted harmonies. If it's ever made into a movie updated to our time, it ought to have Steve Earle and Emmylou Harris doing their Nashville hillbilly version of the Jamaican reggae classic 'Rivers of Babylon' somewhere on the soundtrack:

> Carry us away captivity require from us a song
> How can we sing King Alfa's song in a strange land

Cohen finds the trick of subverting the conventional to comic effect by having Breavman study himself as a narrator imagining himself as a character within his own autobiography. Breavman strives for distance from himself but can't help constantly imploding. He sends himself up serio-comically as both a self-mocked hero and a self-important villain in a story that has multiple orgasms but no climax. The effect is highly visual, dominantly cinematic. Breavman never quite knows what movie he's in but he always knows that there's a camera on him. Several dozen scenes are pure photographs. Here's one:

> He was heading towards Côte des Neiges. The night had been devised by a purist of Montreal autumns. A light rain made the black iron fences shine. Leaves lay precisely etched on the wet pavement, flat as if they'd fallen from diaries. A wind blurred the leaves of the young acacia on MacGregor Street. He was walking an old route of fences and mansions he knew by heart.... He ran to the Mount Royal Hotel. A cleaning lady on her knees thanked him for the mud.

And another – the passage that gives the book its title:

> The juke-box wailed. He believed he understood the longing of the cheap tunes better than anyone there. The Wurlitzer was a great beast, blinking in pain.... It was the kind of pet people wanted. An eternal bear for baiting, with electric blood.... On a napkin he scribbled: Jesus! I just remembered what Lisa's favourite game was. After a heavy snow we would go into a back yard with a few of our friends. The expanse of snow would be white and unbroken. Bertha was the spinner. You held her hands while she turned on her heels, you circled her until your feet left

the ground. Then she let go and you flew over the snow. You remained still in whatever position you landed. When everyone had been flung in this fashion into the fresh snow, the beautiful part of the game began. You stood up carefully, taking great pains not to disturb the impression you made. Now the comparisons. Of course you would have done your best to land in some crazy position, arms and legs sticking out. Then we walked away, leaving a lovely white field of blossom-like shapes with footprint stems.

To put this book on screen you'd have to find a self-mocking Swede with the allusiveness of Ingmar Bergman and the irony of Preston Sturges to .direct it. The New Canadian Library jacket copy blurb says it's 'a shrewd appraisal of the human comedy, where "the favourite game" is love'. No, anybody who thinks that after reading this novel probably thinks Breavman is Leonard Cohen. It's little wonder Cohen looked so gloomy in the seventies: as Breavman says, '[I]n this country writers are interviewed on TV for one reason only: to give the rest of the nation a good laugh.'

Cohen's gloom had more than one cause. Jack McClelland did take his next poetry book but gave the poet a lot of grief. McClelland insisted on changing the title from *Opium and Hitler* to *Flowers for Hitler*, dropping its dedication to 'The Dachau Generation', proposing a cover that featured a drawing of a nude female with Cohen's face for tits before grudgingly accepting a compromise cover featuring elements from six different ones Cohen had designed. Then McClelland published it with a back cover blurb (taken from a letter) that was used against Cohen's express wish. When Cohen remonstrated that 'It was very important that a Jew's book about Hitler be free from arrogant personal promotion,' McClelland responded that the blurb didn't hurt sales. Cohen continued to play McClelland's games: he didn't have many alternatives. He interrupted work on his new novel and went along on a M&S cross-country poetry tour which paid his expenses but made him no money. Cohen complained to McClelland, 'Yankel, Yankel, why did you lie to us?' It took years but he got his revenge. When success as a songwriter allowed him to behave exactly as he liked, he toyed mercilessly with M&S over the production of *Death of a Lady's Man*. Paul Quarrington

142

considers that book 'a novel, and a very good one'. It isn't. To use Cohen's own phrase, it's 'a curious book'.

During his return to Canada in 1963–64, Cohen found himself torn by the conflicts arising from the Quiet Revolution in Quebec. He internalized the contradictions between Indian, French and English senses of nationhood and his own Jewishness and out popped *Beautiful Losers* in two eight-month periods of intense writing and revision back on Hydra. It's a bloody marvel that in 1996 a Western Canadian like Nadel can gloss the politics of *Beautiful Losers* lightly, see them as sources for a couple of scenes and leave it at that because if this book is about anything, it's about the willing of new systems to replace old:

> What is most original in a man's nature is often that which is most desperate. Thus new systems are forced on the world by men who simply cannot bear the pain of living with what is. Creators care nothing for their systems except that they be unique. If Hitler had been born in Nazi Germany he wouldn't have been content to enjoy the atmosphere. If an unpublished poet discovers one of his own images in the work of another writer it gives him no comfort, for his allegiance is not to the image or its progress in the public domain, his allegiance is to the notion that he is not bound to the world as given, that he can escape from the painful arrangement of things as they are.

The words are those of the unnamed Jewish narrator but the ideas are those of F, his mentor, a Québécois MP who has been committed to a prison for the criminally insane because of his anarchist activities on behalf of the separatist cause. The book can be read allegorically as a political fable wrapped inside a sexually transfigured religious fantasy. Hugh MacLennan's 'two solitudes' are replaced by two solitary madmen who keep jerking each other around and off until the beautiful woman meant to unite them is utterly lost through too much history on one side and too much transcendence on the other. As a fable, it's absolutely brutal satire that offers a clearer view of the peculiarities of Canadian repressiveness than anything else written in English in that period: the English are unresponsive to the French but the French are merciless to the Iroquois and the Jews don't do themselves any good.

Before general interest started to wane in the mid-seventies, *Beautiful Losers* was read many ways, not least by Cohen himself. Part of his own list was adopted for the jacket of the first edition:

> Driven by loneliness and despair, a contemporary Montrealer tries to heal himself by invoking the name and life of Catherine Tekakwitha, an Iroquois girl whom the Jesuits converted in the 17th Century, and the first Indian maiden to take an Oath of Virginity. Obsessed by the memory of his wife Edith, who committed suicide in an elevator shaft, his mind tyrannized by the presence of F., a powerful and mysterious personage who boasted of occult skills and who was Edith's lover, he embarks on a wild and alarming journey through the landscape of the soul. It is a journey which is impossible to describe and impossible to forget.... *Beautiful Losers* is a love story, a psalm, a Black Mass, a monument, a satire, a prayer, a shriek, a road map through the wilderness, a joke, a tasteless affront, an hallucination, a bore, an irrelevant display of diseased virtuosity, a Jesuitical tract, an Orange sneer, a scatological Lutheran extravagance, in short, a disagreeable religious epic of incomparable beauty.

Reading this as a put-on by an extraordinary conman, some people found the novel easy to put down and cast aside as pretentious pornography. Until it was 'liberated' from my bookshelves by a former student, I had a signed copy of the first edition. Easy come – easy go. I'd picked it up out of a box of garbage on a sidewalk in Hamilton. Picking up the latest New Canadian Library edition with an Afterword by Stan Dragland, I bemoan my loss even though the cover isn't as shitty as *The Favourite Game*. The first edition sold for $6.50, nearly the same price now as this cheap paperback. In 1966, Jack McClelland priced the first edition a couple of bucks above the market because he didn't want anybody to think M&S was peddling pornography. The loser was Cohen who was forced to settle for a miserly $600 advance. McClelland threw a lavish pre-publication party for 300 and Cohen didn't attend. Sales were poorer than anticipated – not surprising since everyone at M&S seemed more embarrassed than delighted by it. Years later, Cohen hired McClelland as his agent to jerk M&S's tight collars until *Stranger Music* was exactly what he wanted it to be – definitely not a Douglas Gibson book. M&S bound *Beautiful Losers* from Viking's sheets and Viking gave it the quality it needs because Cohen employs a number of typographical oddities that need space to exhale – comic book captions, an advertisement for Charles Axis, a radio transcription of Gavin Gate and the Goddesses, a Greek-English phrase book. These aren't the best things in the book but they're fun.

The best thing about Dragland's Afterword, which is no fun at all – it opens with the assertion that this is 'perhaps the first post-modernist Canadian novel' and then parades all the usual suspect terms of that rhetoric – is that it sent me in search of Michael Ondaatje's 1970 pamphlet *Leonard Cohen*. Ondaatje's essay remains very much worth reading for what he says about Cohen's novels and not just as a key to the evolution of his own. Ondaatje asserts that this is a book that has to be given the benefit of second thoughts. He's right. The first time through, *Beautiful Losers* is simply too sensational, savage, raw, manic. Thanks to Nadel, we now know details of the fasts from food and the sunstrokes, breakdowns, esoteric enterprises, Tantric sex practices, amphetamine overdoses, obsessions with the songs of Ray Charles and other excesses that fed its composition. The amphetamines were diagnosed long ago: this book roars along at chemical-additive freaked-out speed, twists, turns, spins around until you can't miss the point that F is literally correct when he says, 'Hysteria is my classroom.' This book is simply too exhausting to be grasped without subsequent reflection. The question is *'When do you stop?'* I'd say Ondaatje brakes at the right point when he says that *Beautiful Losers* was the funniest novel to appear in a long time, that it takes the notion of *sex as religious liberation* to as extreme a position as it can go and reduces it to a level of absurdity from which it should never have recovered. Exactly.

Writing about a model of sainthood that isn't his own sex practice and doesn't represent his own religious position, Cohen transfigures the vulgar images of Montreal's 'solid bloody landscape' into a wild and peculiar tract. Ondaatje says Cohen lets his imagination ride through the landscape 'like an escaped ski, keeping an incredible balance'. He's right about the balance but wrong about the carriage: Cohen is riding two runaway horses in what looks to me like a reconditioned Egyptian war chariot dedicated to Isis. And he doesn't know how to rein his horses in when they roar out of the west into the spring of Montreal.

> Spring comes into Montreal like an American movie of Riviera
> Romance, and everyone has to sleep with a foreigner, and sud-
> denly the house lights flare and it's summer.... Spring is an exotic
> import, like rubber love equipment from Hong Kong, we only
> want it for a special afternoon.... Spring comes to Montreal so
> briefly you can name the day and plan nothing for it.

The book doesn't end on that unplanned day, it just evaporates into a
fog of Busby Berkeley transcendentalism unworthy of both horses and
rider.

> he greedily reassembled himself into – into a movie of Ray
> Charles. Then he enlarged the screen, degree by degree, like a
> documentary on the Industry. The moon occupied one lens of his
> sunglasses, and he laid out his piano keys across a shelf of the sky,
> and he leaned over him as though they were truly the row of giant
> fishes to feed a hungry multitude. A fleet of jet planes dragged his
> voice over us who were holding hands.
>   – Just sit back and enjoy it, I guess.
>   – Thank God it's only a movie.
>   – Hey! cried a New Jew, labouring on the lever of the broken
> Strength Test.
> Hey. Somebody's making it.

Because the book fails to find its own true ending even by 'renting' the
last page to the Jesuits, I don't think it's as 'incomparably beautiful' as
Cohen asserts. To be this, order has to be restored or chaos must
triumph. Since we're left neither the gold of Jerusalem nor the babble of
Babel but only some bits of Assyrian astrology propped up on a
Hollywood stage, *Beautiful Losers* isn't Cohen's masterpiece as a novelist. That remains unwritten.

In the Winter 1999 issue of the *New Quarterly*, Douglas Glover takes
up the question of why Cohen stopped writing fiction. His essay 'Beautiful Losers' begins:

It's always a mystery why a writer ceases to write, infinitely more mysterious than why a writer begins to write, though perhaps they are related.

I think of Arthur Rimbaud writing *The Drunken Boat* and going off to become a trader in the African colonies, of Nikolai Gogol burning the pages of his sequel to *Dead Souls,* and of the late great French-Canadian novelist Hubert Aquin shooting himself to death after penning the opening pages of a new novel.

I also think of the poet, singer and song-writer Leonard Cohen who wrote two novels – *The Favourite Game* and *Beautiful Losers* – in the early 1960s and then stopped. The latter book, *Beautiful Losers,* is arguably a great novel, an exuberant eccentric: difficult, idiosyncratic, obscene – also gorgeous, prophetic, comic and deeply holy.

After providing an admirably succinct and complete summary of *Beautiful Losers,* Glover analyses Cohen's book as a dramatization of 'the failure of the modern project, the faith or trust in progress, in the improveability of mankind by rational means'. As such, he sees it as standing in the alternative tradition of novel-making that emerged 'through the satires of Juvenal, Lucian and Menippus, through the curious social upturnings of medieval Carnival, to Rabelais and Cervantes and on forward'. Such novels, he writes, are:

comic, parodic, in dialogue with some conventional authoritative form (discourse or language) – this dialogue taking the form of humorous subversion – it is often earthy, bawdy, sexually explicit, if not obscene, blasphemous and revolutionary. It is the voice of the underclass, the marginal and the loser – all thumbing their noses at the toffs in their dinner jackets and fancy dress gowns.

Leonard Cohen's *Beautiful Losers* is a novel in this latter sense, in this alternative tradition. The loser is the winner, the hero is both the villain and a victim of his own heroism.... The reason for these twists, parodies and inversions of conventional form is two-fold. First, Cohen, in the anti-tradition tradition, is drawing the reader's attention to the fact that the assumptions of the conventional novel are simply that – assumptions driven by the bourgeois ideology of down-home realism and common sense. But, second, he wishes to point the mind elsewhere.... Sainthood somehow gets identified with being completely incapable of managing even a toehold on the structure of the modern world. The modern saint, inverting every contemporary value, is muddled, unsure of who he or she is, self-defeating, contradictory, sick and ignorant (and fetishizes his ignorance).

Failure is a double sign. It is a sign of an inability to function in and manipulate the machinery of modernity, but also intimates a different sort of knowledge. The most spectacular version of this is the narrator who cannot narrate, the paradox of a storyteller who cannot tell a story — which some people find a little tiresome but which becomes somewhat more understandable if we conceive it as essentially a religious concept, as paradoxical as the idea of a saint or of God on the cross. The failed poet/storyteller points outside the system to that which cannot be described. He's a limiting concept expressed at the edge of language.

Then, after showing how Cohen uses 'a small anthology of devices' to enliven the novel and subvert modern expectations, Glover concludes:

But from within the system of modernity, a saint and a failure might end up looking the same — sick, dirty, starved and mad — in any event, a complete flop at standardized tests, job interviews, middle management positions and finding a publisher. And what might a true Nabokovian anti-novel look like? The line goes dead. It is possible that, having written *Beautiful Losers*, having in this black romantic and comic tour de force approached the edge, upped the ante and issued a challenge, Cohen realized that there were only two alternatives: repetition or silence. And only one was honourable.

Glover's solution to the 'mystery' of Cohen's silence as a novelist is certainly a 'possible' one but not entirely convincing. What I like about what he has to say of *Beautiful Losers* is that far from being 'post-modern', it stands within an alternative tradition of great antiquity and considerable force. What I don't like about it (beyond all the talk of an indescribable something at the edge of language) is the assertion that there are 'only two alternatives' here or anywhere else in literature or life. That seems to me utterly wrong-headed in itself and false to Cohen's own artistry, which is all about taking third ways and following middle paths. Put another way, it seems to me lacking in respect for both the Jewish and Buddhist elements in Cohen's code of 'holiness'. That's a larger issue than I want to engage here. Jack McClelland was not a devil, but he did give Leonard Cohen as novelist a wickedly bad time: if he hadn't, it's every bit as 'possible' that Cohen would have persisted in writing fiction and ultimately created a work of greater genius and perhaps less ingenuity than *Beautiful Losers*.

In 1976 when Cohen's literary reputation was as high as it ever got, Michael Gnarowski edited *Leonard Cohen: The Artist and His Critics*. Even though he's far grumpier about the novels than I think is just, the best article in it is an essay by George Woodcock, 'The Song of the Sirens: Reflections on Leonard Cohen'. Woodcock's response to the novels is humourless and constricted by his belief that poets ought to stick to poetry. He assumes *The Favourite Game* is autobiographical in ways that it isn't and is so concerned with the aesthetics of *Beautiful Losers* that he overlooks the political allegory. But he can't be faulted in his grasp of the poems, the songs or the sexual politics. Woodcock says Cohen is a good minor poet whose work will last because of his 'sense of the magic of sound in poetry, and ... Yeatsian sense of poetic propriety.' The 'voice for which he will be longest remembered' is the one that records permutations of desire, examines the ambiguities in human response to the universe and sniffs out the sacred in sexual encounters. It's the voice of 'Suzanne Takes You Down'.

In both technique and sentiment, Cohen is deeply conservative as a poet: Woodcock gives chapter and verse and finds the songs even more exaggerated. Cohen's songs, he says, are nothing more than 'the popularization of a conventionally romantic type of verse' that lacks intrinsic feeling. They're essentially empty until life and meaning are simulated by the singer's voice. I can't argue with that: Cohen cheerfully admits that 'Almost all my songs can be sung any way. They can be sung as torch songs or as gentle songs or as contemplative songs or as courting songs.' That's why I prefer tribute albums to Cohen's own recordings. But having said that, I must backtrack: I can't leave it at that. Why? Between

149

writing some of this essay for *Paragraph* magazine and extending it for this book there have been at least a half dozen times when I've found myself inadvertently thrust into a Leonard Cohen song with the compliments of the sound systems in some record shop or bistro: he remains a voice of Montreal. And listening to him by chance, I've found it impossible at least a couple of times not to attend to what he's singing. There are some songs of his – 'Tower of Song' for one – that he so owns and that so own him that a kind of magic happens that doesn't often happen in popular song. It comes from a kind of weariness and seems to succeed all the more for coming out of a damaged instrument. Like some of the cuts that you can find on recordings of Chet Baker and Billie Holiday when they were well past their prime, it has the feel of your own blood and it's utterly devastating.

The success of his songs as escapist vehicles within popular culture has made Cohen far more reactionary than most of his younger fans realize. I haven't tracked his singing career closely enough to determine at what point he unconditionally surrendered to the patriarchal worldview that the best of his early work seems to be struggling to overturn. Or when the original irony of calling his back-up band 'The Army' utterly failed him. But by the early eighties, not only his haircuts and suits but something deeper in him implied a takeover by Ronald Reagan. George Woodcock suggests this was inevitable from the beginning: I have my doubts and my doubts are sustained by the novels. But I have no doubt that Woodcock got to the bottom of Cohen's sexual politics a lot faster than some of Cohen's female friends. Nearly thirty years ago, Woodcock understood that Cohen's loneliness and pain are passive conditions, attributes of a love that gains ultimate fulfilment only in its loss. In Cohen's world, love can be felt but not thought: women are to be looked at, not listened to. As individual intellectual beings, women don't exist and cannot be imagined: they are mere icons, sacred objects to be used in sexual ceremonies for poetic purposes. For some women who like this sort of thing, this is the sort of thing they really seem to like. It flatters narcissists. It pleases sadists and masochists. What it doesn't do is age gracefully. In the final chapters of *Various Positions*, Nadel drools so heavily over Cohen's over-age Don Juanish triumphs over girls living the lives of women and women living the lives of girls that he dodders off without mentioning anywhere that he wrote a previous book about

Leonard Cohen. It's called *Leonard Cohen: A Life in Art* and it's smaller but smarter than *Various Positions*. This is what Nadel writes at the end of its penultimate paragraph:

> In the first phase of his career, life and its ritual symbols formed his art, providing the substance for, and shape of, his writing; in the second, art, as symbolic and religious expression, has fashioned his life.

Criticism is more implied than stated but there's at least some critical element here, some sense that Cohen has ended up as his own best fiction.

Whenever I think about the great novel Cohen's first two portend, I think of a novel as cunning and original as Naipaul's *The Enigma of Arrival*. I think of a work of genius — not ingenuity. But having read Nadel's account of Leonard Cohen's obsessions over the past two decades, I fear it won't ever be written. Cohen has reinvented himself too often to conclude that all he has left in him is the silence implied by 'Jikan' (Silent One), the name he took when he was ordained a Zen monk on August 9, 1996, a position he now seems to have abandoned. But if the only thing left in him is silence punctuated by occasional moments of poetry, it ought to be remembered that before he surrendered so much of his talent to transcendentalism, involvements with women and fictionalizing his own life that he has ended up 'the Bliss Carman of our generation' as John Newlove once described him, he was a novelist, and he's still a novelist to be reckoned much higher than a footnote appended to Michael Ondaatje's career.

So whenever Leonard Cohen is mentioned, I think 'fabulous novelist, ferociously funny, too soon finished' and remember this — from Bliss Carman's 'Envoi' —

> *Success is in the silences*
> *Though fame is in the song*

George Grant at McMaster

Grant himself was never a working philosopher; he was a visionary cultural critic who had a dream of what philosophy might be,
but he never really tried to do the things such a philosopher
would have to do. His mode of agonized pontificating attracted
many readers, who presumably thought that this is what it must
feel like to be a philosopher.

— Francis Sparshott, *The Future of Aesthetics*

George Grant (as I came to know during the academic year 1968–69
when I studied with him) had numerous failings, many of which he
recognized in himself. He sometimes spoke of himself as 'botched and
bungled', by which he meant that his character was flawed in ways that
prevented him from being a philosopher. He was explicit about this. He
was wonderfully explicit (if not always articulate) about everything he
understood and some things he didn't – except when he spoke
privately. In private, his manner was full of what Matt Cohen called
'the strangely unspoken subtexts he provided and opened into'. Cohen
was an instructor in McMaster University's Department of Religion
when I arrived as a graduate student in the summer of '67.

George Parkin Grant was 'towering force in the intellectual life of
this country, perhaps the first truly public intellectual Canada has
produced ... irascible, opinionated and arrogant' as Mark Kingwell
suggests in his January 8, 1994, *Globe and Mail* review of William Christian's *George Grant: A Biography* (1993). Grant died in 1988 after a life-
time spent in teaching, writing and broadcasting during which, Kingwell notes, 'he attacked enemies of wisdom with verve, charm and
tenacity.' William Christian's biography is rich in detail but comes too
close to hagiography for Kingwell's liking: Professor Christian, a political theorist at Guelph, is 'one of a small band of disciples who clustered
around Grant in his later years'. That said, Christian is reliable when he
walks readers through Grant's writings and he does make efforts at
impartiality when reporting Grant's rancorous quarrels with academic

opponents. But, as Kingwell notes, 'he is too much of Grant's own mind to see how prickly and unpleasant Grant could be, how arrogant and unreasonable' and 'takes seriously the suggestion that Grant was a saint'. George Grant behaved at least as rancorously as many of the saints in Butler's *Lives*. But beyond that?

What is beyond dispute is that George Grant was very well connected by blood to the educational élite of Canada's British imperial past. Sir George Parkin, Grant's maternal grandfather, was headmaster of Upper Canada College – a position passed on to Grant's father. George Munro Grant, his paternal grandfather, played a major role in the improvement of Dalhousie University and served Queen's University as its principal. Grant's uncles included Vincent Massey, James Macdonnell and George Ignatieff. His mother called him the biggest *poseur* of all in a family noted for self-dramatization when he abandoned the study of law for theology: in her eyes, he'd been predestined for political office at the highest level.

His family ties did give him a good start on the sort of life that still creates Canada's mandarins. After graduating from UCC and Queen's, he was awarded a Rhodes Scholarship. Nepotism? His uncle Jim Macdonnell was secretary of the Ontario Rhodes committee. Grant was academically gifted but hardly the athletic 'all-rounder' that's supposed to be the Rhodes ideal. At Oxford, he studied law until the Second World War intervened. George Grant was a conscientious objector and the most moving part of Christian's account of his life is of Grant's work as an air-raid precautions warden in the East End of London during the Blitz, providing assistance to victims of the bombing. It was when he was recuperating as a farm labourer in the English countryside that he had the religious experience that was mystical, not sectarian. It provided the foundation for his deeply Platonized Christian faith. In 1985, Grant described it in this way in an interview with David Cayley, reprinted in *George Grant in Conversation* (1995):

I just remember going off to work one morning and I remember walking through a gate; I got off my bicycle and walked through a gate, and I believed in God. I can't tell you more ... I think it was a kind of affirmation that beyond time and space there is order ...

for me it was an affirmation about what is, an affirmation that ultimately there is order. And that is what one means by God, isn't it? That ultimately the world is not a maniacal chaos – I think that's what the affirmation was.

Or, in the phrase he was much given to repeating in the seminar room, 'It was the recognition that I am not my own.'

When the war ended, George Grant returned to Oxford to study theology and obtained a doctorate in it: he had no formal training in philosophy beyond a single undergraduate course. He returned to Canada after he'd obtained an appointment in the philosophy department at Dalhousie when his lack of military service blackballed him at the University of Toronto. Even though his ties to the establishment had served him well, he rejected many of their claims upon him to pursue a life of thinking about what others had thought in the name of philosophy and religion. Beneath an attitude of studious absentmindednss and personal dishevelment that some mistook for worldly unconcern, Grant was ambitious to have a large and direct effect on the post-war intellectual life in Canada as a teacher of philosophy not only in the classroom but also in the larger forums of adult education, newspapers, public radio, and politics. Mark Kingwell, who is in the philosophy department of the University of Toronto and is himself a public intellectual of growing stature, provides this concise summary of George Grant's career in the ranks of his profession in his *Globe and Mail* review of Christian's book:

In 1951, when Vincent Massey chaired a royal commission on the humanities in Canada, Grant managed to secure the task of writing the report on philosophy. He was 33, assistant professor at a small Maritime university. His tendentious opening sentence read: 'The study of philosophy is the analysis of the traditions of our society and the judgements of those traditions against our varying intuitions of the Perfection of God.'

Well, no. It isn't. Grant's lack of philosophical qualifications, together with his devotion to a Christianized version of Plato, has led him astray. The controversy over the report began a career-long hostility between Grant and professional philosophy. It's possible, as Christian suggests, that academic philosophers closed their ranks against him. It's certainly true that Grant kept up a series of attacks against the profession that paid his salary, and reacted with paranoia to the routine politicking of academic departments.

Christian is far from impartial in detailing these skirmishes. It is naughty of him, for example, to repeat a charge that Fulton Anderson, the department chair at the University of Toronto, persecuted Grant because he had rejected Anderson's drunken homosexual overture. Grant knew that it was really by their arguments that ye shall know them. The technical aspects of contemporary philosophy, together with its impatience about religious belief, dismayed him. He thought these traits played into the increasingly technical and money-driven aims of the modern university.

In his *Philosophy in the Mass Age* (1959), a sombre analysis of the efficiency imperatives and progressive dangers of late capitalism, Grant lumped philosophy in with other manifestations of modern technology gone haywire. He even went so far as to resign from the newly formed York University when he was told he could not devote his first-year course to teaching Plato's *Republic*. He would not be startled, perhaps – as I was – to hear that some of my philosophy colleagues have never heard of him.

Grant was by nature a polemicist, and his thought, though often deep, was rarely precise. He took to heart a remark Socrates makes in the course of Plato's Theaetetus that 'too much precision is a mark of ill-breeding.' So though his written work sparkles with insight, it isn't systematic. His positions are hard to pin down and that, predictably, won him many devotees.

Grant never wrote the big book he was continually planning, and he veered from one philosophical enthusiasm to another (now Leo Strauss, now Heidegger, now Nietzsche). Yet his essays, especially in *Technology and Empire* (1969), are models of a good mind in struggle with a world that fights off understanding. His criticisms of modernity and liberalism, now fashionable, were ahead of their time; they remain obscure only because they are so often presented in heavy-handed Christian terms.

Calculated to shock, many of Grant's intellectual formulations lacked subtlety and, especially on the issue of Christian faith, led him to snap judgements.

Philosophically he was a moving target, sliding out of boxes as soon as they were fitted for him. Was he a 'Red Tory', as Gad Horowitz famously said, virulently hostile to the liberal mainstream? Was he a reactionary Christian, railing against nuclear weapons and abortion in the same breath? A Straussian, supplicant of the Western classics? A mystic, devoted to the works of Simone Weil?

Grant was all of these, and more. He was a captivating and bibulous talker, a Socratic companion who broached intellectual topics while deep in his cups, which was often. He was loyal to his friends, devoted to his family, and bitter to his foes. He deeply loved his wife, Sheila, who without credit wrote or co-wrote many of his works. Yet they were given to vicious domestic battles, complete with screaming and air-borne objects.

By the time I met George Grant, he had given up any small claims he might have ever made to being either a philosopher or a teacher of philosophy. The religion department at McMaster where he held the rank of professor offered courses in the 'religious thought' of different eras of various traditions, West and East, and their connections to 'political and social thought'. George Grant was always explicit and articulate on this point: teacher and students together would think the thoughts of the greatest thinkers as accurately as we could as far as we were able. Christian's biography is far sketchier than it ought to be on the early development of the McMaster department after Grant accepted his appointment on the rebound from the debacle of his resignation from York. Christian does not say, for instance, what role Grant had in the hiring of E.P. Sanders (whose renown as a biblical scholar of New Testament and early Talmudic materials is such that every reputable book in that field over the last quarter century refers to him). There is some reason for Christian's silence: E.P. Sanders was at the centre of Grant's later disputes within the department and Professor Sanders, now at Duke, declined to be interviewed.

I first met George Grant when I applied in person to do graduate studies in religion at McMaster: I wanted to study with the author of *Lament for a Nation* more than anything else I could think of doing after I left the seminary. Grant interviewed me right after E.P. Sanders had bowled me over with his great personal charm, accepted my application on the spot and guaranteed me a substantial fellowship. Professor Sanders also arranged supplementary funding that allowed me to start my studies in July and take summer courses in Hinduism before my regular fellowship clicked in with the fall semester.

I'd hoped to begin studying with George Grant immediately, but he was going on sabbatical and passed me along to Louis Greenspan – although not before he'd invited me into his office for what some called Grant's 'head-to-heads'. That's a good term for the kind of encounter James R. Field describes so accurately in 'History, Technology and the Graduate Student: My Encounter with George Grant' in the Spring 1993 issue of *Queen's Quarterly*. Field studied with Grant between 1974 and 1979 and his memories of Grant are more recent, fuller and richer in detail than mine but the essence of our encounters is the same. Grant's one-on-one sessions with graduate students had something of a stage routine about them. Field begins,

> He was a large man with a scruffy grey beard and a shabby coat. His shoes looked like they hadn't seen a brush for umpteen years, and one of the laces was undone. His smile revealed a single lonely fang in an otherwise empty mouth. The fourth and fifth fingers of his right hand, which I took to shake, curled up inside his palm – the result, I was told later, of an automobile accident, making his handshake awkward and tenuous.

Before the accident, Grant's handshake was firm and rather damp. What I remember most clearly of our first encounter other than the physical details of Grant and the 'old tattered chair very much like himself – overstuffed and frayed' (that Field nails, along with the incessant cigarette smoking) was the way he'd greeted my request to study with him with a stare that extended several moments and ended in a question, 'Why would you want to do that?' Field got the same stare and the same question. After I'd stumbled through a long answer of the kind I'd learned to give my superiors during my years in the seminary, Grant urged me to do as he himself had done and be practical and get my graduate degrees with a minimum of fuss. I could confront larger issues once I'd secured a teaching position, he said. He told me he'd written his own thesis on an obscure nineteenth-century theologian of no interest to anyone. He was very solicitous and I was very flattered until I discovered it was the same advice he gave every graduate student who came his way in my day and, from Field's account, for years after:

As Grant continued I grew more and more uneasy and rebellious. What Grant was saying amounted to this: studying philosophy is impractical and can hurt your career. It was the last thing I had expected to hear from him. We had just been discussing truth, faith, madness, and abysses, and he wanted to change the topic and discuss careers!

The essence of this argument was that 'the city and philosophy are at war', a phrase Grant used time and time again. Grant, himself an old trooper and in many ways a casualty of this war, did not want me, or any other of his students, to become casualties as well. As an advisor he was like an overprotective parent, trying to protect his students from dangers they were eager to confront and challenge…. 'Do you want to be eaten?' Grant asked.

The man-eater was the Leviathan, the multiversity – the vanguard of technological society – that the university had become. This was incarnated on the McMaster campus in the nuclear accelerator and 'the Americans' in the religion department in the sixties, the accelerator and the Medical Centre and 'the clever imports from Harvard' in Field's day.

James R. Field and I were both drawn to Grant's seminars by the prospect of studying Nietzsche with him. In this, Field was luckier than I. Grant changed his mind while on sabbatical and, on his return for the fall semester of 1968, was unwilling to offer the Nietzsche seminar he'd announced before his departure. Anticipating that seminar, I'd begun reading Nietzsche on my own. Grant stated we would consider Jacques Ellul's analysis of technology and imperialism instead: Nietzsche was too dangerous. He didn't explain why. I was nonplussed by Grant's reiterated 'He went mad, you know' delivered at the end of lengthening pauses whenever Nietzsche was mentioned either in the seminar room or in private conversations. For his part, George Grant was even more disappointed in me.

During that sabbatical year, I did precisely as he'd suggested and got my M A out of the way faster than anyone had then done in the short history of the McMaster religion department by writing a thesis on an obscure eighteenth-century philosopher-theologian who was interesting mainly because Sir Leslie Stephen, Virginia Woolf's father, had misread him and created a snowball of misunderstanding about the influence of Thomas Aquinas on British natural theology. By following Grant's suggestion to the letter, I'd either failed a test of character I'd not known he'd imposed on me or I'd made things too hot at the graduate studies office for some of his favourite students who'd been longer in the program and had yet to complete their first theses. Or something more abstract and abstruse. Something in me provoked increasing unkindness from him and he never told me clearly what it was. Or I never understood his telling. There was much he said and wrote that he thought I inadequately understood. He was quite right. Despite this, he was the best teacher I've ever had inside a classroom – dramatic and personal, provocative and insightful. He shattered preconceptions and proposed alternative visions. Grant did not 'do' philosophy: he 'taught thought' by thinking out loud what others had thought. Field evokes this by quoting Nietzsche:

You know these things as thoughts, but your thoughts are not your experiences, they are the echo and after-effect of your experiences; as when your room trembles when a carriage goes past. I, however, am sitting in the carriage, and often I am the carriage itself.

My strongest memory of Grant as a teacher is of a Wednesday afternoon when the seminar room in University Hall trembled as he rolled over those who fancied themselves worthy of being his successors. The thinking that matters in our time, he said, is not being done in seminar rooms in Canadian universities or in dons' rooms at Oxford. It is being done in American laboratories – physics buildings, biochemistry buildings, the souls of poets – most probably, in California. Grant spoke of many things but mostly of particle physics that day. He told us all to

take a hike. Literally. He wanted us to look at McMaster's physics building and the nuclear reactor. Both are housed quite subtly in buildings
that don't upset the landscape of the original McMaster campus, a
former Baptist college that once was a nice cluster of Niagara-Escarp-
ment Gothic buildings aesthetically interwoven with winding paths,
extensive grounds and beautiful gardens. The physics building seemed
to be in continuity with the past but was a forewarning of what had
started to come – the big brash concrete blocks of new buildings beginning to dominate the campus of the late sixties. Ultimately, the largest
and ugliest of these, the medical centre, would obliterate one the finest
features of the old campus, the sunken gardens where John Hofsess once
staged the erotic scenes for his split-screen underground anti-war student liberation film *Redpath 25*. The nuclear reactor undermined the
campus in a different way: it hummed, not loudly but constantly. It was
inescapable. A reminder that the physical universe is inescapable, a
fountain of minute energies released by the Big Bang pouring out,
constantly flickering, expanding, scattering a dense and plastic stream
of macroscopic and microscopic events from cosmos to consciousness.

From where I sit today, this dance of flames, the promise of the fire
next time foretold in Revelation and other biblical texts is not now, not
yet, not so near to apocalypse as so many televised evangelists foretell.
Despite them, despite all their assertions, despite the further weight of
New Age religiosity, a procession of sparking particles moving toward a
final fiery meltdown is not the best metaphor for everyday reality. Reality is not really an onward and upward procession that is overtly guided,
continuously and ubiquitously, by extraneous angelic or transcendent
divine forces creating miracles and adjudicating metaphysical truths
that are intrinsically compatible. That is the stuff of verse, not poetry.
From where I sit, life is much harder, closer to the soil of daily experience. God is, to quote Stephen Hawking, the sum of what we do not
know, the ordering principle behind all other principles of order. Reality
is, to quote Paul Shepard, an American ecologist who understands
Heidegger and Marshall McLuhan, 'an unspoken consensus about the
contingency of life and real substructures'. The quotation is from Shepard's essay 'Virtually Hunting Reality in the Forests of Simulacra'. Shepard is writing against Derrida, Rorty, Lacan, Lyotard and other intellectuals 'caught up in the dizzy spectacle and brilliant subjectivity of a kind

of deconstructionist fireworks in which origins and truth have become meaningless'. In his concluding paragraph, Shepard answers those who assert that 'our role as human organisms is to replace the world with webs of words, sounds, and signs that refer only to such other constructions' with the observation that:

> A million species constantly make 'assumptions' in their body language, indicating a common ground and the validity of their responses. A thousand million pairs of eyes, antennae, and other sense organs are fixed on something beyond themselves that sustains their being in a relationship that works. To argue that because we interpose talk or pictures between us and this shared immanence, and that it is therefore meaningless, contradicts the testimony of life itself. The nonhuman realm, acting as if in common knowledge of a shared quiddity, of unlike but congruent representations, tests its reality billions of times every hour. It is the same world in which we ourselves live, experiencing it as process, structures, and meanings, interacting with the same events that the plants and animals do.

Dr Johnson says it more succinctly when he kicks a stone. That's why, incidentally, Mordecai Richler as an astute reader of Dr Johnson is worth reading in ways that Northrop Frye rarely is on any topic and why Margaret Atwood is at her best when she's furthest from the things she absorbed from Frye and closest to the bug-filled life of her entomologist father. When words in the right hands reach and enter the shared quiddity, you can keep transcendentalism in all its guises on the sideboard and I'll make mine a fine wine, immanent with earth, air, water and sunfire.

One hundred years ago, the unifying metaphors that ushered in the twentieth century came from Germany and Austria. The dominant one was the Will to Power. Its poet, its thinker, was Friedrich Wilhelm Nietzsche. Nietzsche did die of insanity as George Grant ceaselessly reiterated but the fatal illness was *atypical general paralysis* most probably resulting from untreated syphilitic infection and not from a surfeit of philosophical analysis. Prior to his final loss of reason, few men have fought as heroically as Nietzsche against this agonizing syndrome, seeking like Job to derive insights from his sufferings.

Nietzsche saw that there is no coherent self, no stable relationship between word and thing, and no fundamental continuity between temporal events. There are simply endless perspectives from which to view events and no boundaries for individuals. Frau Elizabeth Förster-Nietzsche put many words of dubious authenticity into her brother's mouth. However, she may well have been speaking the truth when she claimed that Nietzsche told her how in the Franco-Prussian war of 1870–71, he saw a Prussian regiment continue to attack in spite of immense fatigue, and it was then that it occurred to him that life was essentially not a struggle for survival but a will to power. Writings published in his sane period show that Nietzsche saw it in purely psychological terms at first – that our deplorable tendency to coalesce in herds is a universal all-too-human trait because of fear and our will to worldly power through social success, friendships, influence. Power does not corrupt: it is the will to power that is ruthless and a source of evildoing. The barbarian, the uncultured man, is the least powerful, the most wily and wilful.

Nietzsche moved from an analysis of mass psychology into ethics and a condemnation of moral panic. His later thought wasn't noticed in the way it ought to have been noticed as he moved into the ethical revaluation of all values, especially the Christian ones. Nietzsche (this cannot be repeated too often) never ceased respecting the sincere and genuine Christianity he considered possible for others than himself in every age, including our own. This issue is all too humanly confused with Nietzsche's scorn for the typical Christian's conception of God, a conception that diminishes the value and significance of man with a solemnity that lacks true seriousness. The virtues Nietzsche praises are honesty, moral courage, generosity, politeness, intellectual integrity, self-discipline, hardness, tenderness. His revaluation of values was less a campaign to create new values than a war against the acceptance of conventional behaviour as virtuous in itself. His revaluation included an assertion that the Christianity found in Revelation has more to do with an impotent hatred of enemies, whom it demonizes, than with Jesus's command in the Gospels to love all our neighbours.

Nietzsche became a myth before he died in 1900 due to the considerable propaganda talents of his sister, who patched together some of the thousands of jottings and notes her brother made on his long solitary walks and published the whole mess posthumously as his 'system' in 1901, calling it *The Will to Power*. It supplanted Nietzsche's own title for the last great work illness kept him from completing, *Revaluation of All Values*. By doing this, Elizabeth Förster-Nietzsche laid the foundation for the belief, still current, that Nietzsche's thought is hopelessly incoherent, ambiguous and proto-Nazi, the work of a madman. When I look at the most powerful world nearest to me, the American Empire at the end of the twentieth century, Nietzsche seems wonderfully sane and all too prescient: look at the sense of 'right living' in the American right exemplified by Elizabeth Dole and her legions of Christian Coalition Bible Belles. Isn't their solace in the Bible located in precisely the same place as the certainty of self-righteousness – in Revelation and its attendant apocalyptic dreams and fantasies? Is their understanding of the Bible anything more than a tragic misunderstanding of the human consequences of the 'creative destruction' of the very unfettered American corporate capitalism they so cheerily espouse and George Grant so scathingly skewered in the collection of essays he was honing the year I studied with him, *Technology and Empire?*

In his splendid essay 'Grant's Impasse: Beholdenness and the Silence of Reason' in *Body Music* (1998), Dennis Lee demonstrates that three of Grant's meditations in *Technology and Empire* (1969) – 'The University Curriculum', 'In Defence of North America', and 'A Platitude' – are the heart of Grant's achievement:

Following Heidegger, Grant would now take 'technology' as the most suitable name for the stage which Western Civilization has reached. The term referred to two things at once: the external phenomena which the word usually denotes – machines and inventions and specific techniques; and simultaneously, the stance of mind and will of the society which brought these things into being. Now he could speak in one breath about the external and internal realities of our civilization.... And this gave him a new purchase on issues that preoccupied him. It meant he could situate modern forms of imperialism, progress in science and technology, the doctrine of radical freedom – in fact, a multitude of contemporary phenomena – within a common matrix.... In broad terms, Grant was addressing the problem of modern nihilism.... It was not a question about nihilism *per se*, but rather about our attempts to escape it.... His concern was to give true testimony, however, not to create a detailed taxonomy of mind ruptures.

Grant's testimony is this: 'We are nudged, claimed, inflamed by the good.' He speaks of

things more deeply in the stuff of everyday living which remain long after they can no longer be thought; public and private virtues having their point beyond what can in any sense be called socially useful; commitments to love and to friendship which lie rooted in a realm outside the calculable; a partaking in the beautiful not seen as the product of human creativity; amusements and ecstasies not seen as the enemies of reason.

And Dennis Lee's response is this:

Most of us know such occasions. The sheer ache and delight in a son or daughter's life, which leaves us knowing we're committed for keeps, beneath all calculation and convenience. The way a place corrals us – a patch of Muskoka, a hallowed childhood spot in the back lane. The central *yes* of confirmation when we witness an act of pure integrity, be it public or private. The irrefutable act of desire, let loose by a piece of music. The shudder of recognition when a movement of thought rings true, even though it dislodges convictions we'd hoped to cling to. Who among us has not encountered things we can neither bargain with nor disown? Things to which we are beholden? Things for which, in our best moments, we would go to the wall? This is a knowing that unfolds in a different dimension from anything we hear of in the modern account. And if we are unable to think such knowledge rationally, that does not invalidate what we know.

Grant strove to bring this kind of knowing – these bitter-sweet intimations of good – back to the centre of our attention.

Grant's greatest success was with Dennis Lee and Matt Cohen. And of the two, I think Matt Cohen has made the better artistic use of what Grant had to give. Reviewing Cohen's last novel, *Elizabeth and After* (1999), for the *Globe and Mail* on February 6, 1999, I wrote, in part:

Matt Cohen plays plot, setting, style and characters off one another in a way that delights even as it disturbs. What pulls them together and gives his work a very special beat is a penetrating intelligence that expresses itself with cinematic immediacy. His mind is distinctly his own but he's like the great Australian film director Fred Schepisi (*Fierce Creatures, IQ, Six Degrees of Separation, The Russia House*) in his ability to keep imperfect pasts alive in a tense present and to glide ominously from one to the other and back again without turning everything into a disaster epic. He not only gets under the surface of things in a personal way but understands our social realities, grasps as few Canadian writers ever do that one of the two major differences between this country's ruling class and its underclass lies more in what people drink and who they drink with than anything else. And that the other is the instinctive sense among underdogs that loyalty, that outdated and useless thing that so gets in the way of people and businesses in a hurry to restructure themselves for the global marketplace, is what makes us democrats in our very souls, true not false people.

When I was studying with George Grant in 1968, a year after Matt Cohen had given up teaching in McMaster's religion department to write full time, those of us who sat around his seminar table would hear Grant exclaim 'Matt Cohen – there's a true populist' with an emphasis that left no doubt that the rest of us were more than a little theoretical in that regard. I'd still be envious if *Elizabeth and After* didn't so fully justify that compliment.

My misunderstandings of George Grant were many and varied but I never misunderstood the message of his best-known piece of writing, *Lament for a Nation* (1965). There was never any doubt in my mind that he was talking about the end of Canada as a nation and, with lesser clarity, of the inadequacies in the language of nationalism – political and cultural – to capture and hold the greater good – justice – for which a nation exists. His book was not an appeal for a rebirth of Canadian nationalism. Canada was dead but its remains could be disposed of more or less quickly and we would be better off if we retarded the process of continental political integration for as long as possible: *Residual nationhood is better than none.* That was his message and it still holds even though, in the era of N A F T A, the residue is treated as a persistent stain that must be rubbed out by our political masters. Or, to put it all in the words Grant uses in his 'Introduction to the Carleton Library Edition' of 1970:

The central problem for nationalism in Canada has always been: in what ways and for what reasons do we have the power and the desire to maintain some independence of the American Empire? (It would be impertinent indeed to define what is the chief problem for French-speaking nationalism.) … We are not in that empire as are the exploited colonies of South America, but rather with the intimacy of a younger brother status…. Life as little brother often leads to political naivety and even self-righteousness…. This book was written too much from anger and too little from irony. The ambiguity of the English-speaking Canadian tradition was therefore not made evident. Our hope lay in the belief that on the northern half of this continent we could build a community which had a stronger sense of the common good and of public order than was possible under the individualism of the American capitalist dream…. The sense of the common good standing against capitalist individualism depended in English-speaking Canada on a tradition of British conservatism which was itself largely beaten in Great Britain by the time it was inherited by Canadians. Our pioneering conditions also made individualist capitalist greed the overwhelming force among our elite…. Many Canadians – in church and state and education – worked against this spirit, and hoped to incarnate certain older traditions from western Europe. But one of the reasons their dreams were vain was that they tried to hold on to these things through Britishness, just at a time when western Europe was turning away from its pre-progressive past and surrendering to the same technological Moloch of war and peace which was to reach its height in the u s.

I emphasize this failure in irony because many simple people (particularly journalists and professors) took it to be a lament for the passing of a British dream of Canada. It was rather a lament for the romanticism of the original dream.... We live in an era when most of our public men are held by ignoble delusions – generally a mixture of technological progressivism and personal self-assertion – all that is left of official liberalism in the English-speaking world. *In such circumstances a writer has a greater responsibility to ridicule the widespread ignoble delusions than to protect the few remaining beliefs which might result in nobility ... protecting romantic hopes of Canadian nationalism is a secondary responsibility.* (My italics.)

I suspect that as we as a people become more and more largely underemployed, we'll increasingly find fulfilment in sensuality. Our ability to maintain the distinction between reality and illusion and act upon it will remain in place just as long as we can discriminate between our senses. At the bottom, among the now and forever unemployable of Canada's economic life, we can already see that the boundary lines between the real and the imagined are dissolving to the furthest extent compatible with continued physical survival. Even so, our plight as Canadians is far less complex than that of the citizens of equatorial nations. Their rate of economic progress is much sharper than analysts have ever predicted. They have the potential to overturn the economic card table instead of playing against marked decks distributed by the International Monetary Fund. That's unlikely but it remains a possibility for them. Not so for us. For us, there is no economic alternative to that which is willed by our masters in Washington and we're unlikely to affect their will to power so long as we continue to elect politicians who have America's corporate business interests at heart.

Their will to power. What have we to oppose to the vicissitudes of the multinational corporate world's will to power? George Grant prescribed ridicule and gave us *Lament for a Nation* – a smaller gift than *Technology and Empire*, but a vital one.

Margaret & Philip Surrey, 1975

Of the Streets Where I Live

If on a winter's day I stand up from the desk where I'm tapping this into my computer and step three paces across my office and open the French doors to my balcony and look sharply left up and across the street, I can see almost exactly what a lot of viewers saw when they looked at the advertisements (in the *Globe and Mail* and elsewhere) for the Goodridge Roberts retrospective, which was organized and circulated across Canada by the McMichael Gallery. Posters for that event, which opened at the Montreal Museum of Fine Arts in the spring of 1999, feature a reproduction of 'Studio Window in Winter', an oil-on-hardboard painting made by Roberts in 1957, when he was renting the upper half of a duplex in the row adjoining mine, though which particular unit is a subject of some debate. Philip Surrey, a resident of 478 Grosvenor Avenue for nearly half a century and a painter whose works I prefer to Roberts's, used to point to the one left of centre of four identical row houses some days and the one on the extreme left other times. Margaret Day Surrey, who was Norman Bethune's lover three or four years before she became Philip's wife, used to say that if it wasn't the one left of centre, than it was the one on its immediate right.

From the time we moved onto Grosvenor Avenue in Westmount, Quebec, in the summer of 1983 until they chose to die good deaths a few days apart in the spring of 1990, before their disabilities overwhelmed them, I used to talk to Margaret and Philip separately and irregularly but with some frequency about the people of the streets where we lived. Philip was interested in their sudden moments of unconscious beauty and grace – some of which he captured brilliantly with pastels, less spontaneously in oils. Margaret knew I shared her love of gossip and she gossiped teasingly. She was a great tease and I liked her the more for it that she could still draw blushes from my cheeks. Sometimes I used to tell her that she was the Lili St Cyr of gossips and she'd smile, delighted that I'd compared her to the legendary striptease artist whose body was the first naked female body a lot of Montreal boys saw when they discovered they were men. And maybe then she'd tell me a tale about the artist's model in a certain painting of Philip's who also posed in lesbian tableaux at a private club around the corner from the museum that *tout le haut monde* frequented in the fifties as mixed couples. More often than not, Margaret would open her handbag and produce her most recent letter from her great friend in Paris, Mavis Gallant, and read just a snippet of a remembrance of times past. And leave me wanting to hear more. But I never did hear more than snippets and what she read to me will never be read again since one of Margaret Day Surrey's final acts was to burn all her private correspondence with Mavis Gallant. Margaret deliberately outlived Philip by a very few days only in order to make absolutely certain that what was meant for the national archives and for galleries and for the provisions of their wills went where it was supposed to go and that all that was private was destroyed.

If I stand up from the desk where I'm tapping this into my computer and step those same three paces across my office and open the French doors and look sharply right instead of left, down and across the street from where I live, I can see if the cat is on the front porch at Mary Meigs's house. That cat has appeared in drawings I've seen in various literary magazines. I like those drawings more than I like cats and I like the words they sometimes illustrate even more than the illustrations. I keep meaning to read more of what Mary Meigs has written since what I have read of her relationships with Edmund Wilson, Marie-Claire Blais and others – *Lily Briscoe: A Self-Portrait* (1981) – is full of good gossip and much more art. I sometimes see Miss Meigs on the street but I don't talk to her: she has constructed such a shell of privacy about her that it seems to me brutal to attempt to penetrate it with casual conversation unless you are female and of a certain age. This might be an illusion, an aftereffect of seeing more of her on screen in *In the Company of Strangers* than she allows to be seen on the street where we live. A slight turn of the head leftwards and I can look at the front windows of Ray Smith's apartment. I've read everything Ray Smith has published but not because he's now a neighbour. He has long been a colleague of mine at Dawson College. I read his decidedly odd *Cape Breton Is the Thought Control Centre of Canada* (1969) while I was a graduate student at McMaster University and Ray's story collection was one of those sensational *avant-garde* first books from the House of Anansi. I read his wonderfully original *Lord Nelson Tavern* (1974) when I was teaching in Charlottetown and

I favourably reviewed his unsettling *Century* (1986) before I got to know him too well to review him any longer.

Knowing me and knowing of my interest in the places some local writers inhabit both inside and outside their writings, Ray Smith asked me to give a talk about the writers of Montreal to a group of teachers of English visiting from Denmark in the autumn of 1998. I started my talk by reciting this:

> Suzanne takes you down
> to her place near the river
> you can hear the boats go by
> you can spend the night beside her

For the generation that includes most of those teachers, Ray Smith and myself, Leonard Cohen's 'Suzanne' is likely the best-known of all Montrealers in Canadian literature. Since some people wrongly assume that the Suzanne of this song is Suzanne Elrod, the mother of Cohen's children, I told the visiting Danes that the Suzanne of the song is actually Suzanne Verdal, a dancer who was married to the Montreal sculptor Armand Vaillancourt. She was never Cohen's lover, he insists. And she confirms that it was her choice – not his – that they weren't lovers in an interview she gave the BBC. I also told them that the tea Suzanne Verdal served him along with the oranges was Bigelow's Constant Comment but I couldn't tell them in which building in Old Montreal they'd be able to find her original place by the river: there are several people in diverse buildings who all claim to be living there now, variously gripped by private mythologies I wouldn't want to visit. But knowing that these touring teachers did want to go to Old Montreal, I gave them some general indicators of possible addresses and precise directions to the seventeenth-century Chapelle de Bonsecours, the sailors' church just a little east of the Bonsecours market, where they'd see the source for Cohen's images of Jesus as a sailor. After I told them how to get to Place d'Armes by metro, I read them this passage from Ray Smith's *Century*:

> In a Metro station on a warm Friday evening in springtime. The
> girls, the young women, are going dancing. Some are with

Leonard Cohen at Morton Rosengarten's Vernissage, 1966

boyfriends, some with other girls. They wear clothes in many different styles: neat, dressy, sloppy, weird, colourful, drab, tight, baggy, modest, revealing. (This is the season of punk and preppy, very eclectic; I think the kids are ahead of the designers for once.) The miniskirt is back, along with lots of bright colours like turquoise, red, pink and mauve; hair styles are wild and dramatic; jewelry is big and bright.

The girls are chattering and laughing, their voices singing out in the echoing halls, whispering, while their eyes revolve and wheel, squint and grow large. What are they talking about?

Boys? Boys as suave as Leonard Cohen? They wish! It still surprises me each year that so many of the dancing girls of Montreal who attend Dawson College on the cusp of womanhood still find a shaven-headed, monkish Leonard Cohen, the oldest sixties singer-songwriter in captivity, so inordinately attractive. Not many of them know that Leonard Cohen is not only a singer whose bootleg concert tapes are much prized but also is a fabulous novelist and ferociously funny about the sort of boy he was, the very sort of boy most of these girls in their springtime clothes look at askance when he comes too near – Jewish boys, maybe Cohen's distant cousins, who are too short and too sexually aggressive. Leonard Cohen's novel *The Favourite Game* has wonderful descriptions of adolescence in Montreal that still resonate through later seasons of punk and preppy, seasons of post-punk and post-preppy, and the current season of neo-punk and homeboy Hilfiger neo-prep, eclectic techno and goth. I told the Danish teachers that Leonard Cohen grew up in the neighbourhood of Dawson College and that if they walked west of Dawson along Sherbrooke Street to Clarke Avenue, they'd see a road leading up the mountainside, Côte Saint Antoine, that follows a settlers' trail that follows a more ancient native footpath. Following it, they'd soon come to Shaar Hashomyin synagogue, in which Leonard Cohen had his bar mitzvah. Five minutes further along they'd come to Prince Albert Park, which locals always call Murray Hill. It's fourteen acres, and somewhere buried beneath it are fresh water wells sacred to the original inhabitants of the island, and some of their graves, untouched by archaeologists. The only excavations that take place in this park are in the sandboxes of the children's playground. If they walked into the park

175

and climbed up to the tennis courts, I told them that they'd notice some houses backing on to the west side of the park. The first in the row (599 Belmont Avenue if they went around front to make certain they'd got the right one) is the house in which Leonard Cohen grew up and in which his sister lived until recently. It's also the house occupied by Lawrence Breavman, the protagonist of *The Favourite Game*. Breavman (like Cohen) is fascinated by hypnotism. Whenever I'm near those tennis courts ('Frustrating game, tennis. Keep that wrist straight, oops, missed the sweet spot again,' as Ray Smith writes) watching amateurs will their wrists to straightforward power while playing with fantasies of Wimbledon glory, I remember this scene from the novel: Breavman, in early adolescence, is nearly a head shorter than most of his friends. There's a party. He increases his height with the same technique that Muffin, the girl of his dreams, is said to use to increase her bust: he stuffs his shoes with Kleenex. He dances well for half an hour, but then the wadded paper in his shoes throws him off balance and obliges him to hold Muffin tighter and tighter. It gets a bit passionate. As they walk home, he tells her about his Kleenexes and asks her about hers. She runs away.

> He detoured to the park and raced over the damp ground until the view stopped him. He set down his shoes like neat lieutenants beside his feet.
>
> He looked in awe at the expanse of night-green foliage, the austere lights of the city, the dull gleam of the St Lawrence.
>
> A city was a great achievement, bridges were fine things to build. But the street, harbours, spikes of stone were ultimately lost in the wider cradle of mountain and sky.
>
> It ran a chill through his spine to be involved in the mysterious mechanism of city and black hills.
>
> Father, I'm ignorant.
>
> He would master the rules and techniques of the city, why the one-way streets were chosen, how the stock-market worked, what notaries did.
>
> It wasn't a hellish Bunny Hop if you knew the true name of things. He would study leaves and bark, and visit stone quarries as his father had done.

Good-bye world of Kleenex.

He gathered his shoes, walked into the bushes, climbed the fence which separated his house from the park.

Black lines, like an ink drawing of a storm, plunged out of the sky to help him over, he could have sworn. The house he entered was important as a museum.

That expanse of foliage, those lights of the city, the gleam of the St Lawrence that one sees from the spot where Lawrence Breavman stood are special to me, night and day, every season of the year, and I was pleased to hear later from the Danish teachers that a trio of them had taken the walk to where Leonard Cohen once lived. Some of the others, as I suspected, had gone into downtown Montreal and I'd prepared them for the urban core with a literary introduction to Sherbrooke Street by way of extracts from Hugh Hood's 'Starting Again on Sherbrooke Street' from *Around the Mountain*. They so enjoyed what I was reading about an artist and his friend unloading oversize paintings from the back of a Volkswagen that I lingered longer over Hood's tales of the city than I'd intended and never got back to much that I'd prepared for these visitors – selections from Clark Blaise, Daniel Richler, Norman Levine, Ann Diamond, Robert Majzels – before turning to my own stories of this city on an island in the middle of a river in the muddle of a partially paved, partially cleared forest in the Laurentian mountain range, Westmount and my own route to Murray Hill.

From where I live on the lower, less fashionable part of Grosvenor Avenue near the commerce of Sherbrooke Street, I have to walk uphill to get to Murray Hill Park. The hill is steep and I'm asthmatic and until my bronchodilator kicks in, my breaths are short and my pace is slow. But I was also raised on the Prairies and climbing hills of any description never comes naturally to me. Philip Surrey came to Montreal from Winnipeg but his route was circuitous and covered half the world and even in his late seventies he had good wind for this hillside. In the last months of their lives, as Philip became more and more depressed and disoriented over the loss of sight in the eyes that had always meant so much to him, Margaret Day Surrey edited an account of her husband's life that was deposited in the National Archives of Canada at his death. I hope, one day, to turn it into a book: Philip's stories are growing dim in my own memory – they ambled and meandered in a Prairie boy's way and his artist's tone, feeling and image tended to overwhelm linear narrative. Margaret was more hesitant to speak of her past but when she did, she established facts in a less forgettable way. And her past – she was seventy-something when I first met her but did seem much younger – and memorable. Patricia Whitney has posted a memorial on the Internet 'First Person Singular: Margaret Day Surrey' and says of it, 'I have written the tribute for three reasons: because the impact of Margaret's personality was very great; because, while the stories of the men associated with *Preview* have been told, her story has been ignored; and because she, and women like her, represent the crone in our literary history.' Margaret would have been irritated to see herself described in print as a crone and Philip would have teased her for it while tacitly agreeing that there was something substantial and true in what Whitney means when she writes, 'The crone is a source of wisdom and power for all women and for the men who will hear her voice.' Margaret loved and was loved passionately and even at eighty-something when Patricia Whitney interviewed her in the summer of 1989, 'Her movements were quick and neat, her cultivated voice vibrant and full of humour.' And immense, unguarded sexiness. Margaret phoned our house once when I was out and did not leave her name because her call had to do with a surprise I was arranging for Ann's birthday. Ann who spoke to her often in person but never before on the phone didn't recognize Margaret's mechanically enhanced velvet fog. When I did get home, Ann definitely wanted to know who the mysterious lady with the bedroom voice was and wasn't best pleased when I wouldn't say – not until her birthday. Margaret was hugely amused and quite proud that her voice was still an instrument to rouse ire in a much younger woman.

In 1933, Margaret's father had sent her to London to study voice at the Royal College of Music. Before the year was out, her father died and everything was gone of the family fortune. On her return to Montreal, she taught school in one of the poorer parts of Montreal, her brother died of tuberculosis and her sister was hospitalized for it. Margaret turned to Marxism, travelled to Russia, came back to Montreal and met Norman Bethune who had treated her brother at the Royal Victoria Hospital. Bethune was forty-six, Margaret was twenty years younger:

he was her first lover and she became pregnant and he performed the abortion before he left for Spain in October 1936. In January 1938, just when Bethune was leaving for China, Margaret met Philip and they married a year later and moved in to the house at 478 Grosvenor Avenue and lived there for nearly fifty years.

There's not nearly enough written about Margaret and Philip Surrey and 'the set' of painters and writers they belonged to in the forties and fifties when social life in Montreal was dominated by 'sets'. Among others, that 'set' included F.R. Scott, Marian Dale Scott, John and Corrine Lyman, Patrick and Peggy Anderson during the war years and Mavis Gallant and Brian Moore after the war. Within the set, Margaret was important in the genesis of *Preview* – the anti-Fascist poetry magazine – and in the nurturing of the writerly ambitions of both Moore and Gallant. After the late and very great Brian (then pronounced *Bri*-rhymes-with-*fly*-an) Moore gave up his newspaper job to write full time, he lived just two streets east of Grosvenor at 498 Lansdowne Avenue, and used to drop by for coffee in the mornings and hand Margaret freshly typed pages to read. And then they'd discuss them. She was the first person other than the author to read the early novels. Knowing how much I like *The Luck of Ginger Coffey*, parts of which Moore had mailed to her from New York while he was writing it, some days when we met in the street, Margaret would test me in her teasing way by just saying its opening words to see if I was paying attention, 'Fifteen dollars and three cents'. If she hadn't caught me totally unawares, I'd reply, 'He counted it and put it in his trouser pocket.' And then we'd chat for five or ten minutes and then she'd be off again. Philip once told me precisely whose jaunty Tyrolean hat with 'the two Alpine buttons and the little brush dingus in the hatband' Ginger Coffey was given to wear in the novel but I have forgotten the owner's name and remember that hat's dingus as Philip sketched it on the air as he said, 'Phallic symbol'.

The set to which the Surreys belonged, like many other smart sets along the eastern seaboard, got caught up in Freudian psychoanalysis after the war. Philip was fascinated and Margaret was particularly vulnerable to talk of Oedipal complexes and processes of repression. Throughout the fifty years of their marriage, Margaret suffered recurrent sieges of depression. Was that 'the price she paid for stifling her

Philip Surrey with Gabor Szilasi, 1983

own creative nature'? That's Patricia Whitney's verdict, not mine. Whitney writes that Margaret told her

> that she realized that if her husband were to be able to paint, given his 'artistic temperament' and his chronic drinking, then she must subsume her ego to his and create for him the kind of oasis of calm where his talent would emerge. She did this, giving up her own dreams of writing.... Evidently, she felt that Philip's success was the vindication of her decision. Such a judgement seems bizarre in the contemporary social climate, but Margaret Day Surrey was born and nurtured in the patriarchal age. Given her times and circumstances, she acted with sensitivity and love.

When Philip Surrey drank, I suppose he drank heavily: many artists of his generation were that way inclined. Gabor Szilasi and Doreen Lindsay who lived across the street for thirty of those fifty years remember Philip best for the sensitivity and love with which he cared for Margaret after she'd undergone her 'treatments' up at the Allan. Margaret's depression, she told me, predated Philip and persisted despite him. And if a judgement on their past is to be made by the standards of the present, it ought to be levelled more against that age's 'abstraction' than Philip's gentle realism. Here is one of the best descriptions of Montreal under the spell of modernism:

> He began his tour through the heart streets of Montreal. The streets were changing. The Victorian gingerbread was going down everywhere, and on every second corner was the half-covered skeleton of a new, flat office building. The city seemed fierce to go modern, as though it had suddenly been converted to some new theory of hygiene and had learned with horror that it was impossible to scrape the dirt out of gargoyle crevices and carved grape vines, and therefore was determined to cauterize the whole landscape ...
>
> He turned and looked at the city below him.
>
> The heart of the city wasn't down there among the new buildings and widened streets. It was right over there at the Allan, which, with drugs and electricity, was keeping the businessmen

sane and their wives from suicide and their children free from hatred. The hospital was the true heart, pumping stability and erections and orgasms and sleep into all the withering commercial limbs. His mother was sleeping in one of the towers. With windows that didn't quite open.

And that too is from Leonard Cohen's *The Favourite Game,* a coming-of-age novel that captures both a young man and his city at moments of profound transition.

Those moments continue in the young who pass through Dawson College and in the older buildings of its neighbourhood. When Ann and I first came to live in Westmount in May of 1974, we lived at Number 24, The Melbern Apartments, a pre-war building at 335 Clarke Avenue that is down the block, around the corner and three blocks over from what was then the Mother House of the Congrégation de Notre Dame and is now Dawson College. Two blocks east of Clarke and one west of Dawson is Greene Avenue where we used to shop for groceries at the Steinberg's on Greene Avenue that's now called Cinq Saisons. Greene Avenue has always attracted ladies with powerful appetites for shopping and shops with attitude to service them. Art galleries, antiques emporia, haute couture salons and bathroom fixtures boutiques now dominate a street that in the mid-seventies still displayed a lot of neighbourliness with flashes of sixties counter-cultural and college life. A row of gingerbreaded townhouses – destroyed by fire some years ago – housed the then-funky progressive rock radio station CHOM, which attracted a lot of cultural icons and oddities. Daniel Richler was often to be seen there when he wasn't taking classes at Marianopolis College or hanging out with his girlfriend at Dawson College's student radio station, lower down Greene Avenue, in the converted pill factory at 350 Selby Street that was then the main college campus. I used to see him yo-yoing between the two places, maintaining cool by acting unfriendly and disconnected. It didn't work very well – he had too much energy, too much innate charm. Like his novel, *Kicking Tomorrow* (1991), a book I regard more highly than anyone else I know. It's not merely well crafted, it's alive and lively with well-observed moments. Here's one: it's St Jean Baptiste Day in 1976 and the book's eighteen-year-old protagonist, Robbie Bookbinder, has been to Mont Royal for one of those now-legendary Fête Nationale concerts held then and he's back in West-mount and in Westmount Park, the third and largest and most public of my city's green spaces:

> In the middle of Westmount Park was a brightly painted booth equipped with a sound system, known in the neighbourhood as the Kiosk. There was a concrete clearing around it, with blistered wooden benches, provided by the municipality to keep all the trouble in one place. Across the park, past the swings and library on Sherbrooke Street, you could always hear the supreme heav-iosity of guitar riffs, whumping out over the trees.
>
> It was mostly Anglo-Quebeckers who gathered there, West-mount High students, famous in the city for the achievement of being perpetually stoned.... These cats just liked to hang out, revving their bikes, perching on the back of benches like patched-up parrots, smelling of patchouli and savage B.O. They smoked joints and grooved, sunlight flashing off the little mirrors embroidered into their Indian-cotton frog shirts. And the main thing was that to maintain your cool, you had to act unfriendly. You had to sit there looking like a Strolling Bones album cover, just being a lizard with a sewed-up mouth, sitting in twilight, in the crack between worlds, Castaneda-wise, not releasing a drop of emotion. Now Robbie wondered why he'd come. He looked around him with a sinking heart. He'd been so *up* until he saw these long faces, these indolent bystanders, these pseudo-hippies gone prematurely to seed, still waiting, he observed sourly, for another generation's revolution, still playing someone else's old romantic records.... Like, six blocks over and a short hike up the hill Canada's coming apart, it's having a revolution all of its own, *and none of these turkeys even knows about it.*

Daniel Richler was a far more frequent sight on the streets of West-mount than his father. In those days, Mordecai Richler and family lived at 218 Edgehill Road on the upper, toffiest side of the Boulevard just below Summit Park and the top of the hill after which the city is named. I didn't speak to him when I saw him squeezing tomatoes at Steinberg's or even when I was seated three feet from him in Smither's Shoe Shop as he purchased a pair of brogues. Or anywhere else when chance put us in the same public place at the same time. That happened rarely. People who live on the upper reaches of Westmount spend summers across the river in the Townships, the Richlers on Lake Memphremagog. The easiest to meet, most friendly of the Richlers was Mrs Richler: I mean the *elder* Mrs Richler, Mordecai's mother. Mrs R. ran a rooming house just above the railway tracks that Selby Street is below. I met her while shopping for used furniture from an advert in *The Examiner,* Westmount's weekly newspaper. She had a chest of drawers for sale that one of her tenants had left behind in lieu of rent. I didn't buy it but she insisted on giving me a glass of lemonade and introducing me to another of her tenants and before I knew it a couple of hours had slipped by and I'd gained a memory that's still as lively as this one recorded by Norman Levine twenty years earlier, in 1956. Levine made a trip across Canada and out of that trip produced *Canada Made Me.* It was published in England in 1958 but only a few copies were circulated in Canada by the uncourageous McClelland & Stewart until it was finally published by Deneau and Greenberg in 1979, a less than illustrious reception for what is one of the best works of literary non-fiction that has been created out of Canadian experiences. Levine has just come in by train from Halifax:

We landed in Montreal near midnight; a blizzard was blowing. I decided to get as quickly as I could to Ottawa, to my parents, and shake off whatever it was that I had caught, then plan and begin the journey. But there wasn't a flight out until tomorrow. I rang Mrs R. She had a rooming house in Westmount. I was grateful that her son in London had written to let her know that I was coming. She said that all her rooms were taken but that a Greek girl was away for a few days and I could sleep in her bed.

It was a narrow wooden house, high, undecorated, with a steep outside staircase, the steps icy and covered in snow. A secluded dead end street opposite a playing field and by the railway tracks. The house beside it was exactly the same, in the front window a sign ROOM TO LET. I knew this area, a kind of no man's land. It had a good address but it was hidden halfway between the wealth of Westmount and a slum.

Mrs R was a small Jewish woman with a harsh nasal voice. She reminded me of a small bright bird, a sparrow. It didn't matter what she said, she made it all sound like a comedian telling jokes. As long as she was talking she appeared confident. It was only when she was a listener that one noticed the vulnerability; the melancholy look in the eyes, the clumsiness of her generous gesture. She had placed on the kitchen table a leg of cold chicken and some sliced tomatoes; but I wasn't hungry. While I was telling her news of her son, a girl came in. Mrs R introduced her as Rosemary, the German girl from upstairs. She was in her middle twenties, straight blonde hair down to her shoulders, coarse features; she looked as if she'd been used by other people. The face was pale, shy, defensive, and the generous body had started to lose its shape, her belly pushed out from the brown skirt that was too tight and too short. But one could feel immediately a heavy, lazy sensuality emanating from her. And with it an innocence, a kind of trust, that asked to be violated. She said she had arrived fifteen months ago from a small town in Southern Germany. Her only contacts, so far, were at night school. She said she didn't like Montreal, she wasn't meeting enough people. I started to cough again and they both became concerned. Rosemary, who spoke a broken English, said she knew a German recipe which was good for colds, fever and the grippe. Mrs R brought out lemons and honey and Rosemary made strong tea and then mixed all the ingredients together. Then another occupant of the house came into the kitchen. He was thick and graceless in a drab secondhand blue suit that was too small for him. He grunted good evening, the face unshaven, sullen, and fat. He went to the refrigerator, took some food from his allotted corner, grunted again and went out. Mrs R said he was a Latvian who had been with her for the past ten years. 'My boy friend, he can't leave me,' she said and laughed without much amusement. 'He's got only one passion in life and that's food. He'll keep stuff under his bed that's so rotten it's growing things. And the stink when I open his door. But ...' and the shrug that followed, the hunched narrow shoulders, said eloquently, that's the way with the world: 'He's always first with the rent.' I could hear a gramophone playing in the room next to the kitchen and a distant squeaky voice: 'When the sun has gone to rest, That's the time we love best ...'. 'That's Frank,' Mrs R said 'He's a mechanic with an aircraft factory and he gets records and papers sent over from Scotland. The guy's been over here two years and he's still homesick.' We listened to Harry Lauder coming through the thin wooden partition. Rosemary stood awkwardly by the sink, then with a shy sleepy smile said good night and went upstairs. As soon as she had gone Mrs R told me that Rosemary had just had an illegitimate child, that she was anti-Semitic, that she had no job, and was broke. 'I'm sure that if our roles were reversed and she was in my shoes and I was in hers she would have kicked me out long ago.' How easy it is to tell recommended strangers intimate details of one's life when you know there's no responsibility to be faced. We talked on. She told me of her operations, showed me the gallstones kept in a small glass jar; that she used to work in a nightclub but was now working in a respectable clothing store 'for a couple of gangsters'.

Elsewhere in the book, Levine writes 'I like the lower towns, the places across the tracks, the poorer streets not far from the river. They represent failure, and for me failure here has a strong appeal.' Levine's observation of the physical squalor and intellectual poverty behind the economic optimism and social complacency found everywhere in Canada evokes both George Orwell and Henry Miller and ranks with their best work. When I read the first edition copy of *Canada Made Me* I found in the Westmount Library in 1975, I thought it was the best piece of writing about Canada I had ever read. I still feel the same way. And it kicked me into starting to write and to write every day of lives lived in Regina and Hamilton and Halifax and Ottawa and Montreal and England and elsewhere.

When I started to write fiction in 1975, Westmount was home to three fine writers. There was Mordecai Richler high up the hill and Clark Blaise and Bharati Mukherjee at the De Maisonneuve end of Clarke Avenue, the second house in from the corner, 4297 De Maisonneuve Boulevard West. Although I passed both of them in the alleyway behind their townhouse several times a week as I came and went from college and they bundled their sons in and out of the family Audi at the beginning and end of schooldays, I never introduced myself. That seems odd to me now, as odd as not speaking to Mordecai Richler: I know now what I didn't know then about writers and that is that there isn't one of us alive who isn't delighted to hear words of praise from a reader who *genuinely* admires their work. In retrospect, I think in those days I was silenced by my own ambitions, that I only wanted to meet other writers when I could meet them not as a reader but as a fellow writer with some claim to equal status, at least with the claim to having a book of my own in print. If I had stopped and spoken, words of admiration would have flowed more freely for Bharati Mukherjee's novels *The Tiger's Daughter* (1972) and *Wife* (1975) than for Clark Blaise's story collections *A North American Education* (1973) and *Tribal Justice* (1974). That's partly because I only wanted to write novels then, paid longer fictions far closer attention than I gave short stories. But something of it also has to do with a reverse snobbery, my radical distaste for stories that have the stamp of the University of Iowa Writers' Workshop (or any other creative writing program) on them. They too often seem to try just a little too hard to exert charm as if to apologize for their extreme cautiousness. In this, I now think I was projecting the faults of Blaise's students at Concordia University's writing program on to his own work. Even his talented students were far too reverential, too uptight about formal perfection, too goddam aesthetically neo-Platonic for their own good, forever searching out moments of pure illumination and transcendental self-realization that you've got to be a W.P. Kinsella to believe in. Brighter minds are silenced: Terence Byrnes was probably Blaise's most talented disciple at Concordia and Byrnes has published one small, fine collection of stories, *Wintering Over* (1980), and afterward seems to have given up writing fiction altogether in favour of instructing others – he's the current chairman of the Concordia writing program.

My attitude towards what Blaise is doing in his own work began slowly to move in a better direction when I read *Days and Nights in Calcutta* (1977), the dual account of a lengthy stay in India written by Blaise and Mukherjee. His journalism here and in *The Sorrow and the Terror: The Haunting Legacy of the Air India Tragedy* (1987) is rich in social and cultural detail but it also highlights his compassion for the victimized, the outcast and the outsider, his humanism. But it was reading *I Had a Father: A Post-Modern Autobiography* (1992), his blending of genres to present the mystery at the heart of his storytelling, that has led me in recent years to really rediscover the artistic power of his short stories. In this, I hope I'm at the leading edge of a developing trend. Blaise is a very good writer, one of our best. The passages I wanted to read to the Danish teachers are these, taken from 'Extractions and Contractions' in *A North American Education*:

THE DENTIST: My teeth, my body, my child, my wife and the baby she is carrying are all in the hands of immigrants. All Jews. I do not know how this develops; because I am an immigrant too, perhaps. Our friends warned us against the indigenous dentists. Between hockey pucks and Pepsi caps, they said, Quebec teeth are only replaced, never filled.

This dentist's office is in a large, formerly brick office building that was stripped to its girders over the summer and then refaced with concrete panels and oblong windows. Inside, however, not a change. The corridors are still reminiscent of older high schools, missing only the rows of olive drab lockers. The doors are still darkly varnished and gummy from handling. The doctors and accountants still have their names on stippled glass. All this, according to Doctor Abramovitch, pains a dentist, whose restorative work is from the inside out. 'Rotten inside,' he snorts, poking my tooth but meaning the building. He is a man of inner peace, rumoured to be a socialist. The rest of our doctors are socialists. His degrees are in Hebrew but for one that puzzles me more, in Latin. I am in the chair waiting for the freeze to take effect before I realize that Monte Regis means Montreal. I then remember a novel I have just read, a French-Canadian one, in which the narrator, a vendor of hot dogs, must decide on a name for his hot dog stand. The purists suggest *Au roi du chien chaud*. He chooses *Au roi du hot dog*. The author, I am told, is a separatist. I wonder if he cares that at least one outsider has read him. Poor Montreal, I now think, puts up with so much.

There is a battle this afternoon to save a tooth.

ST CATHERINE STREET: From the dentist's, east on St Catherine is an urban paradise. No finer street exists, in my experience, even in November. St Catherine should be filmed without dialogue or actors, just by letting the crowds swarm around a mounted camera and allowing a random sound track to pick up the talk, doppler-ing in and fading out, from every language in the world.

But west on St Catherine, especially in November, is something else. Blocks of low buildings after Guy Street, loan offices on top and business failures down below. Auto salesrooms forever changing franchises, drugstores offering two-hour pregnancy tests, news and tobacco stands, basement restaurants changing nationalities. But if it can be afforded, or if one lives only with a wife, a convenient location. Someday Montreal will have its Greenwich Village and these short streets between St Catherine and Dorchester will be the centre.

I stop at an unlighted tobacconist's for the papers. One window bin is full of pipes and tins of tobacco, the other of dusty sex magazines from every corner of the Western World. The owner stands all day at the door and opens it only if you show an interest. Otherwise, it's locked, without lights. I stop in daily for my *Star* and *Devoir*. I always have two dimes because he keeps no observable change. He always responds, '*Merci.*' His face implies that he has suffered; also that he survives now in his darkened store by selling far more than the *Star, La Presse,*, and all the Greek and German stag magazines. I have seen men enter the store and say things I couldn't understand and the owner present them with Hungarian, with Yiddish, with Ukrainian, with Latvian papers. Then they chat. Perhaps he speaks no English and just a word or two of French. Like my dentist, a man, ultimately, of mystery.

I selected these for the visiting teachers because they highlight social and cultural details that I thought would interest them, reflect small similarities and large differences between Montreal's downtown and Copenhagen's.

Several weeks after speaking to the Danish teachers, I gave a reading at Westmount Public Library as part of a series marking the library's centenary. After reading from my own work in progress, I took my audience on a literary tour of Westmount by reading selections from Leonard Cohen, Daniel Richler, Norman Levine, Clark Blaise and Ray

Smith – I closed with a passage in Smith's *The Man Who Loved Jane Austen* where Frank, the man of the title, walks through Westmount Park and passes very close to the spot depicted in Daniel Richler's novel, a spot about three hundred feet from where I stood reading.

Darkness had come by the time Frank stepped out the door. But even now, in late August, the evening air was soft as he made his way along de Maisonneuve and into Westmount Park. To his right the last of the shrieks sounded from the swimming pool, and under the lights the tennis courts were busy. Frustrating game, tennis. Keep that wrist straight, oops, missed the sweet spot again. Culp had a game the day I was there, so there are tennis courts in Port Simcoe, Jonathan should be learning the game, maybe even Simon. Along the pathways, through the trees, he saw people strolling with their books fresh from the library, couples strolling in the pools of lamplight, in the clouds of nicotiana scent, stopping to embrace. Away to the left, the traffic of Sherbrooke Street, and beyond it the mountain with the glimmering of its houses rising to the dark trees of Summit Park. Jonathan nine, Simon five, and he had never taken them for a walk in Summit Park. The pool, the playground off beyond the watercourse, the soccer field, Family Day here also, but never to Summit Park, only once to Mount Royal Park on the main mountain – what a narrow life he was giving them. Perhaps in Port Simcoe. Surely it wasn't really happening. His terror of change was precariously balanced by his exhilaration at the idea of leaving. But how peaceful this evening. Only when you knew where to look could you see on the trees the damage from the ice storm. What stranger, strolling here like this now, could guess at the devastation of January? What stranger, strolling here like this now, could guess at the continual dull turmoil of life here? And what turmoil, really? Dull was the word. It's not Omagh, not Kosovo. As a few years ago they used to say it's not Belfast, Beirut, Sarajevo, Rwanda. And most unlikely it would ever be like any of those places with their bombs and machetes – we had the Supreme Court decision. Everyone said it – the PQ would likely win the election again and lose the referendum again. And then it would go on the same old way again. He had lived with it these twenty-five years and more – why go now? Why indeed? Mordecai Richler was staying – why shouldn't he?

After the reading, I fielded questions and observations. Someone said, 'I don't like reading things set so close to where I live. I like books to take me to places where I've never been.' I was startled. I'm frequently startled by reactions from the audiences at my readings. I suppose if I wasn't, I wouldn't have the heart to do any at all. Live audiences alert writers to unvoiced assumptions: We come to love the good by first loving our own as Dennis Lee notes in his essay 'Grant's Impasse' in *Body Music*.

By first loving our own! I still remember the little click as that phrase slid into place, and I realized I actually knew what he was talking about. Grant was giving me back my love for those pines, that rocky shoreline, the ramshackle cottage – giving it back in a luminous further dimension. For it was true: this was not just a casual attachment. To be claimed by that boyhood place of the heart, so deeply it almost hurt – that was inseparable from who I was. And it made sense. It was right. Loving our own is what human beings *do*. At the same time, giving my heart to that little patch of ground was something to grow ahead from. It had schooled me in the homing of desire, prepared me to love less immediate forms of (all right) 'the good'.

The Westmount in which I live and teach and read and write are for me what 'those pines, that rocky shoreline, the ramshackle cottage' on a lake north of Toronto are for Dennis Lee: the artists of these streets have 'schooled me in the homing of desire.'

Philip & Margaret Surrey, 1975

Choosing the Best

In the final appendix to *The Western Canon*, Harold Bloom engages in 'a mug's game' of cultural prophecy and lists what he considers to be the likeliest contributions of the 'Chaotic Age' – the twentieth century – to the Western canon. His list of nearly twenty double-column pages is arranged by country of origin. Canada's contribution comes somewhere between the West Indies and Australia in brevity. Bloom asserts that he has 'neither excluded nor included on the basis of cultural politics of any sort' but admits that his list 'reflects some accidents of my personal taste'. From Canada, he includes

Malcolm Lowry *Under the Volcano*
Robertson Davies *The Deptford Trilogy* and *The Rebel Angels*
Alice Munro *Something I've Been Meaning to Tell You*
Northrop Frye *Fables of Identity*
Anne Hébert *Selected Poems*
Jay Macpherson *Poems Twice Told*
Margaret Atwood *Surfacing*
Daryl Hine *Selected Poems*

This is a list free of cultural politics? Maybe, but if it's free of academic politics, Bloom's personal taste is very accident-prone indeed. Bloom gets things about as badly wrong about literature in English Canada as any American ever got anything about Canada but he does get one thing wonderfully right: Bloom makes no mention of the novels of Margaret Laurence.

Canadians too can get things badly wrong about their own literature: in lists of 'canonical' Canadian books that have appeared since the Conference on the Canadian Novel was held in Calgary in 1978, Laurence's *The Stone Angel* either appears at the top (as it did at Calgary) or is displaced from top spot by *The Diviners*. What's wrong with that? In the first place, neither represents Laurence's own best book – that's *A Jest of God*. In the second place, a lot of what Laurence wrote, *The Diviners* pre-eminently, belongs to the realm Bloom labels 'period pieces' – works 'as imaginatively dated now as they were already enfeebled when they first came into existence'. In the late and least productive part of her working life, Laurence made much of herself (and was made much of by those writers who thought of themselves as members of her 'tribe') as 'a figure of moral conscience to her fellow writers and a spokesperson for the integrity and efficacy of art in our society'. So writes Professor J.A. Wainwright in his introduction to a selection of letters of Margaret Laurence, *A Very Large Soul*.

In a rejoinder, 'Margaret Laurence: Soul Woman', in his collection *Ripostes*, Philip Marchand takes up some of the odd things that do happen to the imaginative capacities of a writer such as Laurence who doesn't make a radical separation between her life and her art and becomes her own 'artwork' – the loss of any sense of irony, the desire to out-moralize moralists, and an ever-increasing and rabid sentimentalism over the non-human. In her memoir *Dance on the Earth*, Laurence writes, 'How dare we call our species *Homo sapiens*? The whales and dolphins, whom we are rapidly destroying, are surely superior in every way that counts.'

Marchand is as fair as fair can be in his response to Laurence's novels:

Even her best novels suffer from a certain banality. To be sure, *The Stone Angel* and *A Jest of God* are good novels. Laurence's speciality was the evocation of pathos, particularly with respect to characters who, for one reason or another, feel themselves to be comical or pitiable outsiders in small-town Canadian society. There are times when this evocation becomes very affecting. One of the more piercing moments in her fiction, for example, occurs in *A Jest of God*, when the heroine's mother, thinking of her long-dead husband, murmurs half-consciously, just before falling asleep, 'Niall always thinks I am so stupid.' The reader feels instantly the rightness of this small episode and can share the heroine's dismay at the thought of how many times the old woman has tortured herself with the reflection. It is a fine touch, and more disturbing in its way than, say, the more obvious trials of Hagar Shipley.

Indeed, it's an accumulation of fine touches and small disturbances that come to the reader (with little of the advance telegraphing that mars *The Stone Angel*) that makes *A Jest of God* Laurence's best novel. This is some of what the London publisher Carmen Callil and the Irish writer Colm Tóibín write of it in *The Modern Library: The 200 Best Novels in English since 1950* (1999):

> *A Jest of God* is a monologue written in the present tense by a teacher in her mid-thirties who lives with her mother in a fictional town in Canada. Within one or two pages Margaret Laurence creates a complex emotional landscape and a voice which is perfectly pitched, so that her material, which may seem unpromising to certain readers, becomes intensely interesting and memorable.
>
> The progress of Rachel Cameron, her constant fear of her colleagues and her boss, her extraordinary sensitivity to what is going on around her, to each nuance of right and wrong, are described in a way which is exact and real ... Rachel's summer love affair with an old school friend, which is the dramatic core of the book, is riveting; at times you have to put the book aside for a while, so tense is the emotional atmosphere, so full of challenges and possibilities. *A Jest of God* is a small masterpiece.

It's certainly good, masterful and superior in every way to Laurence's attempt at a masterpiece, *The Diviners,* which was published eight years later. In *A Jest of God,* Laurence places Rachel and her mother in a flat above a funeral parlour. The regular references to death below them is an attempt to add a deeper significance to Rachel's tale that it doesn't need. It's so unnecessary in fact that readers can ignore it and not lose much. Unhappily, readers can't ignore the defining symbol in *The Diviners* – 'the river of now and then' – a river flowing in two different directions that parallels the novel's construction as the narrative flows back and forth between the past and present of Morag Gunn. Here's Philip Marchand on Morag's current state:

> It's a life story that loses intensity the older the heroine gets and the closer she comes to McConnell's Landing. By the time she

arrives in McConnell's Landing she has become a figure suspiciously similar to ... Artwork ...

A significant portion of Gunn's McConnell's Landing reflections are, in fact, devoted to writerly problems. ... Unfortunately, these sound like the musings of earnest unpublished writers who are faintly pleased with themselves for being so dedicated to their craft. They have the tone of that good advice given to novelists in writers' magazines with articles entitled, 'Yes, It Sounds Like a Lovely Metaphor – But Ask Yourself Is It Something You've Really Seen?'

Morag's reflections on the writing life are silly and self-indulgent. They undermine the book's moments of strength by calling attention to the author's own inability to attain the level of narrative she controls in *A Jest of God*. Near the end of his essay, Marchand remarks of *The Diviners*:

No wonder Grade 13 English departments like this novel. There are a lot of essay topics here. Explain the River of Now and Then. Compare and contrast Christy's Work in the Nuisance Grounds with Royland's Work as a Diviner. What is the Significance of the Phrase, 'The train moves west,' as it is Used throughout the Novel?

Staring drop-mouthed at the list of books that have made it on to *Quill & Quire*'s 'Forty Great Works of Canadian Fiction' (*Quill & Quire*, July 1999), I kept wondering how many were there just because they're full of essay topics – topics that can be assigned to students and topics that can be turned into essays on Canadian writing to be delivered at meetings of professional societies and published in academic journals so that their authors progress up the slippery slope of scholastic success rather than perish.

Quill & Quire asked thirty-seven people – some academics, some writers, some booksellers, and some librarians – to submit nominations for 'the 30 most interesting, important and influential' books of Canadian fiction of the 20th century 'published in English between January 1, 1900, and December 31, 1998'. *Q&Q* editors 'selected the 50 titles that received the greatest number of votes' out of 270 put forward for consideration and asked panellists 'to rank this shortlist of fifty titles in order of preference.' The panellists were:

Gailmarie Anderson	Ajay Heble	Ruth Panofsky
Mary Jo Anderson	Allan Hepburn	Marianne Scott
Richard Bachmann	Aritha van Herk	Stephen Smith
Donna Bennett	Thora Howell	David Staines
Eugene Benson	Renée Hulon	Fraser Sutherland
E.D. Blodgett	Lorna Jackson	William Toye
George Elliott Clarke	Janice Kulyk Keefer	Alan Twigg
Verne Clemence	Richard King	Thomas Vincent
Ian Colford	Alma Lee	J.A. Wainwright
John Robert Colombo	Donna McKinnon	Diane Walker
Nathalie Cooke	Holly McNally	Bruce Whiteman
Sarah Ellis	George Melnyk	
Carole Gerson	Elaine Kalman Naves	

By my reckoning, sixteen of the thirty-seven are academics. And the survey said:

1. *The Stone Angel*, Margaret Laurence (1964)
2. *The Wars*, Timothy Findley (1977)
3. *As for Me and My House*, Sinclair Ross (1941)
4. *Fifth Business*, Robertson Davies (1970)
5. *The Apprenticeship of Duddy Kravitz*, Mordecai Richler (1959)
6. *Lives of Girls and Women*, Alice Munro (1971)
7. *Who Has Seen the Wind*, W.O. Mitchell (1947)
8. *Sunshine Sketches of a Little Town*, Stephen Leacock (1912)
9. *The Diviners*, Margaret Laurence (1974)
10. *Anne of Green Gables*, L.M. Montgomery (1908)
11. *Obasan*, Joy Kogawa (1981)
12. *The Double Hook*, Sheila Watson (1959)
13. *The Mountain and the Valley*, Ernest Buckler (1952)
14. *The Stone Diaries*, Carol Shields (1993)
15. *Green Grass, Running Water*, Thomas King (1993)
16. *Beautiful Losers*, Leonard Cohen (1966)
17. *The English Patient*, Michael Ondaatje (1992)

18. *Under the Volcano*, Malcolm Lowry (1947)

19. *In the Skin of a Lion*, Michael Ondaatje (1987)

20. *By Grand Central Station I Sat Down and Wept*,
    Elizabeth Smart (1945)

21. *Fugitive Pieces*, Anne Michaels (1996)

22. *A Fine Balance*, Rohinton Mistry (1995)

23. *The Temptations of Big Bear*, Rudy Wiebe (1991)

24. *Such a Long Journey*, Rohinton Mistry (1991)

25. *The Handmaid's Tale*, Margaret Atwood (1985)

26. *Coming Through Slaughter*, Michael Ondaatje (1976)

27. *The Watch That Ends the Night*, Hugh MacLennan (1959)

28. *Swamp Angel*, Ethel Wilson (1954)

29. *Two Solitudes*, Hugh MacLennan (1945)

30. *Such Is My Beloved*, Morley Callaghan (1934)

31. *Who Do You Think You Are*, Alice Munro (1978)

32. *Tay John*, Howard O'Hagan (1939)

33. *The Lost Salt Gift of Blood*, Alistair MacLeod (1976)

34. *Surfacing*, Margaret Atwood (1972)

35. *Not Wanted on the Voyage*, Timothy Findley (1984)

36. *St. Urbain's Horseman*, Mordecai Richler (1971)

37. *The Edible Woman*, Margaret Atwood (1969)

38. *Bear*, Marian Engel (1976)

39. *Home Truths*, Mavis Gallant (1981)

40. *From the Fifteenth District*, Mavis Gallant (1979)

My jaw wasn't the only one to drop. *Quill & Quire* reported that some of the panellists were less than enthusiastic about the final results. Here are some of the reactions *Q&Q* printed:

'My god, it's so conservative it could campaign for Mike Harris. I'm disgusted at it. Unless there's some mechanism that really did permit the unusual, the interesting books to come through, you end up with the lowest common denominator. I think it's a reflection of how Canadians like to smooth things out. We like to take the middle ground. If I were going to look at it optimistically, I guess we should be grateful for these grandmothers and grandfathers. The genealogy is firmly in place. Now let's get on with it.' – Aritha van Herk, the University of Calgary

'This list shows that the books we consider important are the books we were taught. We put *Who Has Seen The Wind* on there – I didn't – but we don't ask, for example, how much it's influenced other authors.'

        – Renée Hulan, Saint Mary's University

'It tells me there's really no fresh thinking going on, that we're not in a great moment critically.' – George Melnyk, the University of Calgary

'It's a deep truism that the only way B.C. fiction gets acclaim or notoriety is if it's published by an Ontario publishing house. That's a real problem, and it's only reflected in a list like this. All these authors have to leapfrog out of where they live. It's a real drain. It's not that the fix is in, it's no Machiavellian plot, it's just the way it is.'

        – Alan Twigg, editor of *Bookworld*

'I think any way you try and adjust it to balance out, say, regions or genders, you're just going to skew it in another direction.'

        – Gailmarie Anderson, the Melfort Bookstop, Melfort, Sask.

How difficult is it to apply fresh thinking that hasn't been 'adjusted' to balance out regions or genders, that doesn't put us back in the classrooms of our youth, that doesn't worry about political categories such as conservatism or its opposite, that doesn't just strive to be 'interesting' or 'unusual'? Surely it isn't that difficult to determine what's the best that Canadian writers have written? At least, I've not found it so and neither, it seems, have Callil and Tóibín. They state in the introduction to their *The Modern Library: The 200 Best Novels in English since 1950* (1999):

> Enthusiasm is the driving force of this book. Its purpose is to celebrate the writers we have loved best, and to proselytize on behalf of their novels: sources of entertainment and enjoyment as satisfying as any Hollywood movie, football match, computer game or rock video. We recommend these novels, not for their academic interest, or their illustration of the theory of the death of the author (an invention, in Carmen Callil's opinion, of academic literary critics with not enough to do to pass the time), but for precisely the opposite reason – for their illustration of the very

life of the author, the power of the live voice, the passion to tell a story, invent characters and find a form.

Their inability to be entertained cheaply or satisfied easily and their common enthusiasms for the right things – the power of the live voice, the passion to tell a story, the invention of characters and discovery of form leads them to include the following Canadian books. Their listings are alphabetical by author:

Margaret Atwood, *Alias Grace* (1996)
Robertson Davies, *Fifth Business* (1970)
Mavis Gallant, *From the Fifteenth District* (1979)
Margaret Laurence, *A Jest of God* (1966)
Alistair MacLeod, *The Lost Salt Gift of Blood* (1976)
Rohinton Mistry, *A Fine Balance* (1995)
Brian Moore, *Black Robe* (1985)
Alice Munro, *Friend of My Youth* (1990)
Michael Ondaatje, *In the Skin of a Lion* (1987)
Mordecai Richler, *St Urbain's Horseman.* (1971)

Now that's a list that's that gets several things absolutely right and is worth discussing in its entirety for the pure pleasure of coming to grips with voices, stories, characters and forms!

Margaret Atwood, *Alias Grace* (1996). In 1991, Brian Fawcett argued in his essay 'Margaret Atwood's Achievement' from *Unusual Circum-stances, Interesting Times* that it was time to 'assess Margaret Atwood's skills as a mature writer and not as a shit-kicking *enfant terrible*.' And what he says on this score is 'she's grown, and what one encounters in *Wilderness Tips* is a different writer than the one we read even a decade ago. She still has the hard-edged persona and confidence, and a similar but enhanced technical and intellectual virtuosity. But she's more gener-ous now, less bitchy, and her focus has a truly marvellous depth and patience.' All this is true and it might be no more than an accident of personal taste – my distaste for *faux* nineteenth-century settings no mat-ter how well done – that leads me to assert that *Life Before Man* (1979) is Atwood's best novel and *Alias Grace* takes second place. *Alias Grace* is remarkable for its form and Atwood's ability to treat sexual encounters enigmatically. It's witty, mysterious and full of human paradoxes. But so is *Life Before Man* and it has dinosaurs and Toronto as palpable presences. Some readers complain that it's too cold and prickly, but the 'sexual revolution' of the sixties wasn't warm and fuzzy. Anyone with doubts on that point really must read Fawcett's own telling *Gender Wars* (1994).

Robertson Davies, *Fifth Business* (1970). *Fifth Business* is Davies' best book and the only one I'll ever recommend to anyone who feels obliged to read him. Callil and Tóibín comment that 'its stilted style is in contrast with the deep pain which is buried in the narrative, and the play between the two is often breathtaking and always engrossing.' If Davies hadn't added two more volumes to turn *Fifth Business* into the first volume of the Deptford Trilogy and demonstrate that he was incapable of writing in anything other than a stilted style or inventing any voice, male or female, that wasn't Dunstan Ramsay's, I'd be more tempted to celebrate his achievement here. I'd still place *Fifth Business* somewhere near the bottom if I was asked to do a *Quill & Quire* list of my top thirty. Having read more of Davies than is good for anyone, I'm of the opinion that reading him ought not to be encouraged at all. Because of a peculiar interest in the doings of High Church Anglicanism, I confess I might one day be tempted to have another look at his second-best novel, *The Cunning Man*. I can't think of anything that would ever lead me to re-open the pages of Anthony Burgess's favourite Davies, *The Rebel Angels*.

Mavis Gallant, *From the Fifteenth District* (1979). Mavis Gallant's range is astonishing and her writing is impeccable. In no other single volume has her wit, intelligence and unique sharpness been better displayed. If I could have only one uncollected volume of her stories, this would be it. Since *The Selected Stories of Mavis Gallant* does exist, I don't have to settle for less: it's one of a very few essential story collections of this century. Not enough can ever be said of the power of Gallant's narrative voice, her uncanny ear for dialogue, which rivals Dickens' in reportorial skill, her inventiveness of forms, or indeed of her emotional range and depth as a storyteller. Her comic abilities range from caustic wit to lampooning satire. When it comes to Mavis Gallant, words fail me in ways they never fail her.

Margaret Laurence, *A Jest of God* (1966). A small masterpiece.

Alistair MacLeod, *The Lost Salt Gift of Blood* (1976). MacLeod was born in 1936 and has published two books of seven stories each, newly released in one volume as *Island* (2000), and the current bestselling novel, *No Great Mischief* (1999). This is the better known collection, one celebrated by a great many academics: MacLeod has spent years and years teaching English and creative writing at the University of Windsor. His writing is probably as close as any Canadian has ever gotten to the James Joyce of *Dubliners*. MacLeod deals effectively in raw emotions between parents and children and the landscape of Cape Breton. This is a first-class book of short stories, but I can think of a trio off the top of my head that are as carefully crafted and as emotionally effective and accurately situated – Bonnie Burnard's *Women of Influence* (1988), Mary Borsky's *Influence of the Moon* (1995), Clark Blaise's *A North American Education* (1973) – and I'm only up to the B's. I'd rank Ray Smith's *Century* (1985) – a fellow Cape Bretoner's utterly different and more difficult book – at least equal to MacLeod's in literary elegance, and Smith never glides into sentimental excess. MacLeod does. That apart, this is a small masterpiece.

Rohinton Mistry, *A Fine Balance* (1995). Unlike Alistair McLeod, for instance, Rohinton Mistry brings something other than emotional power and technical mastery to the older traditions he works within. Mistry's talent doesn't just lie in applying exact observations à la Dickens-Tolstoy-Balzac to the subcontinent of India. He writes political novels that owe something to Zola but are unmistakably of the twentieth century. I don't think this is his best novel simply because his abilities haven't peaked. Like Mavis Gallant, who was among the first to recognize his enormous potential, he'll really flower in his mid-fifties – somewhere around 2005. If readers remain responsive and Mistry remains his lovely self-deprecating self, he's going to keep us in fine new books throughout my retirement years. Lucky us. Lucky me.

Brian Moore, *Black Robe* (1985). Which do you like best – early, middle, or late Moore? I have a particular fondness for *The Luck of Ginger Coffey* (1960) but recognize that *Judith Hearne* (1955) is more accomplished.

Anthony Burgess thought *The Doctor's Wife* (1976) particularly brilliant and I agree. But Moore's greatest skills are found in the terser political novels of his third phase: *Black Robe* is a dark and deeply disturbing book, truly haunting. I revere it in spite of this. Moore's best writing is all about conflicts surrounding loyalty and belief because he has an uncanny knack of getting inside convictions many of us find alien. The universe of the natives is rendered with such force in *Black Robe* that every time I take it up I quite forget that *Catholics* (1972) remains the Moore novel no one else could ever have written.

Alice Munro, *Friend of My Youth* (1990). People who continue to pump Munro's *Lives of Girls and Women* to the upper rungs of the CanLit canon and – worse – continue to teach it to college students at this late date really do get up my nose. For two reasons. Better textured, more fully layered collections of interlinked stories of girls growing to womanhood in ways more central to more young lives – once again, Mary Borsky's *Influence of the Moon* comes immediately to mind – have surpassed Munro's. There's nothing surprising in this since Borsky is only one of many who have learned from it. The larger reason, of course, is that Alice Munro, like Mavis Gallant, reached artistic maturity in her fifties and found new ways of placing large fictions in short stories. I don't have a favourite Munro collection, just a stack of stories I admire. Most of them appear in *The Selected Stories* of Alice Munro.

Michael Ondaatje, *In the Skin of a Lion* (1987). Callil and Tóibín write that Ondaatje's 'genius is in creating one of the best novels of the century about work, which is also one of the best novels about dreams and disappearances and magic.' I wish I could say the same because this novel tries so very hard to be worthwhile in just those ways. The problems I have with Ondaatje here – apart from the carefully deliberated tone, which turns the mind to jelly if you let it – is that he seems to get the main form of work he considers – bridge-building – wrong in uninteresting ways. I'm never confident that he actually knows what he's talking about. I'm not alone: the word on the street is that engineers tend to hoot derisively when they read it.

Mordecai Richler, *St Urbain's Horseman* (1971). It's not enough to say, as

Callil and Tóibín do, that 'Jake Hersh is one of the great Jewish creations of the North American novel' because this novel is as much English and European as North American. And its great success at being utterly Jewish makes it thoroughly human. Jake Hersh and his world belong with the great fictional creations of the English language. Period. Exclamation point. The fact that this is not widely recognized in Canada more than saddens me, it makes me deeply ashamed of the teaching profession.

Carmen Callil and Colm Tóibín selected only 194 novelists for their book *The Modern Library: The 200 Best Novels in English since 1950*, because they wanted to give readers the chance to contribute to the list. What would I add? Mordecai Richler's *Solomon Gursky Was Here*. Absolutely. There are also days when I'm tempted to follow Anthony Burgess's lead and add in Richler's *Cocksure* – but I won't get into that.

Mordecai Richler, *Solomon Gursky Was Here* (1989). This is the closest anyone has yet come to writing the Great Canadian Novel. It has social scope and historical sweep, it's funny in all of the ways Canadians ought to find helpful in living through the Brian Mulroney-Jean Chrétien years. Richler is even more ambitious here than in *St Urbain's Horseman*, and very nearly as accomplished.

Leonard Cohen, *The Favourite Game* (1963). What's more typically Canadian: struggling to elevate yourself to the middle class or falling out of it in disgust with what you find there? These days, after a quick count of body piercings and tattoos in any of my classrooms, I'd say the latter pattern is more prevalent, but favourite stereotypes are slow to die. Whenever establishment-minded WASPs – look again at chapter 7 of Atwood's *Survival* – take it into their heads to contemplate eastern Europeans or Asians in Canada, they find Duddy Kravitz everywhere. Some days that's almost reason enough to forget how good a novel Richler's *The Apprenticeship of Duddy Kravitz* actually is. Much as I love Richler's work, Stephen Vizinczey's *In Praise of Older Women: The Amorous Recollections of András Vajda* (1965) is a fresher novel about a young man in a hurry to get somewhere. Leonard Cohen hung out with Vizinczey and learned a lot by seeing the world through his eyes.

Cohen's artistic vision is under tighter control here than in *Beautiful Losers*, the CanLit critics choice. *The Favourite Game* captures both a boy and a city moving into a new and fiercely modern age with even greater ambivalence and a more excoriating view of male sexuality than Richler manages. A small masterpiece which might prove even larger if anyone gets around to publishing the version McClelland & Stewart wouldn't touch. Cohen writes a poet's prose: this is not to be confused with the 'poetic prose' of Anne Michaels, Michael Ondaatje and Jane Urquhart – it's a much finer and rarer music.

Hugh Hood, *Around the Mountain: Scenes from Montreal Life* (1967). The city that's a secondary character to Larry Breavman in Cohen's *The Favourite Game* is front and centre here in a way that no Canadian city has ever been at the heart of a book.

Rudy Wiebe, *The Blue Mountains of China* (1970). Wiebe was born and continues to be a Mennonite. *The Blue Mountains of China* is something like a collection of short stories and something like an episodic novel but really it's as *sui generis* as Hood's *Around the Mountain*. Wiebe covers a century of Mennonite history – the migrations from Soviet Russia to Canada and Paraguay – as a sequence of various forms of Christian faith and action. It's a remarkable vision. Because the characters are German-speaking Christians who see themselves in biblical terms, everything – including Wiebe's syntactical indebtedness to his Low German mother tongue – works to a common artistic end. Wiebe is frequently celebrated in this country for his novel *The Temptations of Big Bear* (1973) which just doesn't work because he imposes Old Testament archetypes on native characters in ways that are credible only if you accept his biblical faith. Even if you do, the language of the characters doesn't ring true. Low German was widely spoken in the Midwest after the Civil War but it didn't have quite as pronounced an effect on common English language use among tribesmen as Wiebe suggests.

So here's my answer to Carmen Callil and Colm Tóibín's Canadian selections and most of my answer to Harold Bloom. At the end of the twentieth century and the beginning of the twenty-first, what's *most* worth reading among books by Canadians that contribute most to the

Western canon? In alphabetical order, I say

Margaret Atwood, *Life Before Man*
Leonard Cohen, *The Favourite Game*
Mavis Gallant, *Selected Stories*
Hugh Hood, *Around the Mountain: Scenes from Montreal Life*
Brian Moore, *Black Robe*
Alice Munro, *Selected Stories*
Mordecai Richler, *St. Urbain's Horseman*
Mordecai Richler, *Solomon Gursky Was Here*
Rudy Wiebe, *The Blue Mountains of China*

That's it – these nine – no others? Nothing from the West Coast? Well, I certainly won't add Malcolm Lowry's *Under the Volcano*. To quote Robert Fulford, whom I'm otherwise unlike, 'I decided long ago that either Lowry and his disciples were nuts or I was.' Howard O'Hagan's *Tay John*? O'Hagan is as good at following in the wake of Joseph Conrad's *Nostromo* as MacLeod is in following *Dubliners*. *Tay John* is a very ambitious first novel, but without really feeling any need to make a list that shines from sea to sea, I'll include one book from British Columbia –

Emily Carr's *The House of All Sorts* (1944). Emily Carr is Emily Carr and *The House of All Sorts* is an account of her life as a landlady and raiser of sheep dogs. Carr wrote of herself with the same clarity and directness with which she painted the world around her. She heralds a 'new' way of looking that's, in fact, very eighteenth-century and 'enlightenment'. Carr's writings point in many directions all at once – not least to a long-standing symbiotic relationship between visual arts and literature in this country that's rarely examined as closely as it ought to be. Emily Carr was an original 'jest of God' – an artist and writer who became, in her time, a measure of things Canadian, a lightning rod for the philistines and misogynists who are forever doing their damnedest to make this country and its populations small and petty and sexist. Carr's responses in the shape she gave words on the page no less than the lines of her painting express that which is always worth fighting for – not merely against – in life. In this, she's a perfect friend to the characters found in these other eleven books and a companion to any of us who call upon her.

Carr's work is non-fiction and Harold Bloom includes a work of non-fiction by Northrop Frye. I'll not flatter any literary critic or public thinker so much but there are two more non-fiction books that accomplish necessary efforts of imagination that none of our fiction writers have succeeded in doing as consummately.

Norman Levine, *Canada Made Me* (1958). While people like Hugh MacLennan and Morley Callaghan were attempting to write Great Canadian Novels, Levine went out and lived his way through one. My idea of hell of earth would be to go anywhere with Norman Levine as a travelling companion. But his very unsympathetic nature is what gives the writing a rare kind of life. As travel writing and lived experience, this is the equal of Henry Miller and George Orwell even though Levine has neither Orwell's political sense nor Miller's sexiness. Casually brilliant.

As is damn near everything he's written. I'm especially awed by the stories in Levine's *Something Happened Here* (1991) and his novel *From a Seaside Town* (1970).

Brian Moore, *The Revolution Script* (1971). Moore thoroughly denounced and did his best to discredit and disown this book in his later years. He thought he'd been totally misguided in his attempt to create a 'docudrama' about the kidnapping of James Cross by the FLQ in Montreal in 1970. Obviously, I don't agree. The students who fomented social revolution throughout the Western world in the late sixties and early seventies were often silly, self-serving and far too smug in their approach to violence. Moore treats his small band of urban guerrillas with a surprising degree of sympathy, without denying their stupidity, because he sees more deeply into the contradictions at the heart of our society than most of us ever do.

And that's it? A mere dozen.

There's nothing mere about any of them. These twelve books have much in common with one another and little in common with the generality of books that get published. Each, in its own distinct way, is built upon the power of a lively and enlivening voice. Each has stories that demand to be told and are told with passion. They create characters who are both familiar and strikingly odd in their responsiveness to others. And each author gives a new shape to experience, registers a significant shift in contemporary consciousness as it reacts to new circumstances. Because each of these books does all these things to a remarkable degree, they can't be exhausted in one reading. They insist on staying with us and furnishing our minds. What these books don't do is construct a cultural 'national dream' to rival the old CPR's commercial enterprise. These books aren't built for 'tourists' to admire and 'boosters' to put to 'nationalist' political ends. They are discontinuous with the length and breadth of this country and its full social history. Collected together, what they tell us about our country is that it has generally been indifferent to the economic fortunes of its writers and that more writers have found refuges in Montreal and Toronto than elsewhere. What they demonstrate about how literature furnishes our lives is something else, something so glorious that it makes me a close observer of their visions and of those who continue the 'traditions' they work within.

List of Photographs

All photographs, including the cover and page 212, are courtesy of documentary photographer Gabor Szilasi. Since arriving in Canada in October 1957, Gabor Szilasi has dedicated himself to extending the boundaries of the documentary tradition in still photography. As a photographer and as a teacher, he has influenced a generation of artists and earned international recognition for his clarity of vision tempered by remarkable kindness. *Gabor Szilasi: Photographs 1954–1996*, a collection of his work, has been published by McGill/Queen's University Press.

Photographs appear on the following pages:

About the Author

T.F. Rigelhof was born and raised in Saskatchewan. Since 1973, he has lived in Montreal where he teaches ancient literatures at Dawson College and writes. He also serves as a contributing reviewer to the Books section of the *Globe and Mail*. His essay on religion in Canada at the end of the millennium, *A Blue Boy in a Black Dress: A Memoir* (Oberon, 1995) won the QSPELL/Royal Bank of Canada Award for Non-fiction in 1996 and was nominated for the Governor General's Award. He is also the author of two novels, *The Education of J.J. Pass* (Oberon, 1983) and *Badass on a Softail* (Goose Lane, 1997) as well as a collection of short stories, *Je t'aime Cowboy* (Goose Lane, 1995). He lives in Westmount, Quebec.